NATIONALISATION

# Nationalisation

compiled by Temba A. Nolutshungu

First published **January 2011** by **Free Market Foundation**

Second edition **June 2011**

Edited by **Joan Evans**

Research for case studies by **Gavin Ray**



**Johannesburg** | PO Box 785121, Sandton 2146, South Africa
TEL 011 884 0270 | FAX 011 884 5672 | EMAIL fmf@mweb.co.za

**Cape Town** | PO Box 805, Cape Town 8000, South Africa
TEL 021 422 4982 | FAX 021 422 4983 | EMAIL fmf.ct@mweb.co.za

**Websites** | www.freemarketfoundation.com | www.healthpolicyunit.org

**ISBN** | 978-1-874930-88-4

Printed by Intrepid Printers (Pty) Ltd - 4354

NATIONALISATION

# Contents

# Preface

## Temba A. Nolutshungu



This publication has three important purposes. They are:

1. To disseminate and make generally accessible the facts and empirical arguments in the debate on the policy of nationalisation and to address the moral dilemma of socialism.
2. To provide information to those who feel uncomfortable in principle with the policy of nationalisation and perceive the potential harm that could be done to the economy if the policy proposed by the ANC Youth League is adopted and carried through.
3. To engage with those who support the policy of nationalisation on a philosophical and intellectual level.

To do all of this, this study must be relevant from the imagined perspective of a reader in Khayelitsha, Soweto, Mitchells Plain or Melville, which I believe it is. Of course, in some cases, the reader might have to pause to think through what is being said. I believe also, that, right now, this is exactly the effect such a study should have.

For the first 23 years of its existence, the FMF argued, cajoled and pleaded for the total dismantling of the apartheid system and the establishment of true democracy in South Africa, with universal suffrage and a constitution that would highlight the principle of limited government, so as to protect the people from ever again being the victims of the pernicious policies of arbitrary government, such as the discriminatory laws that deprived people of their rights because of the colour of their skins.

It is consequently with great sadness that we find ourselves addressing a proposal to nationalise the mines, a proposal which invokes racialism and calls for some of the most important aspects of the Constitution to be tampered with in pursuit of an economically unsound political objective. This study is a sincere attempt by the FMF to argue, cajole and plead once again for good sense to prevail.

The authors of the various papers contained in this study are committed to contesting the doctrines held by those who propose the nationalisation of mines in South Africa. While the writers focus upon the debate surrounding nationalisation in South Africa itself, the arguments they present have a global relevance and resonance and are backed up by sound historical and empirical evidence that brings into question the morality of the underlying doctrines, as well as their practicality.

The approach is succinct, cogent and reasonable and is, therefore, accessible to all who are interested in the debate. This includes direct stakeholders in targeted industries as well as anyone who is concerned about policy matters that have serious implications for the country.

We have to ask ourselves how this proposed law, regulation or policy is likely to affect the ordinary people of our country, especially the young, old, poor, unemployed, or otherwise vulnerable. In the FMF, this question is always at the back of our minds, whatever issue we may be trying to address. We believe that no measure can be good for the nation in general if it threatens to bring about negative consequences in the longer term for the vulnerable members of society, however well-intentioned it might be. Proposed policies, whatever they are, have to be very carefully considered because, as this study reveals, the long-term negative consequences of a proposed law, regulation or policy are not always immediately apparent and are very difficult to reverse. Finally, the crux of this study is about the perpetual struggle between imposed ideology and the spontaneous order of free markets and economic freedom.

This study consists of six freestanding chapters, each with an executive summary, dealing with various aspects of the nationalisation debate. The reader can therefore select what to read and the order in which he or she wishes to do so. In addition, this preface provides a brief overview of the chapters so as to make it even easier for busy readers to home in on what interests them most.

## Analysis of the ANC Youth League's Nationalisation Proposals

In Chapter 1, Leon Louw, Executive Director of the Free Market Foundation, audaciously interrogates the reasons why the ANC Youth League (ANCYL) wants to nationalise mines and other businesses. This leads to a thorough and objective analysis of the *Freedom Charter* and its intentions; an examination not only of the wording of the *Charter* itself, but also the comments and explanations of the senior members of the ANC who were involved in its drafting. It also leads to a paragraph-by-paragraph analysis of the ANCYL's documents, which support the nationalisation proposal. The conclusions are surprising and, some might believe, controversial. Whatever readers may conclude, they will recognise that the analyses are thorough and dispassionate; the work of a seeker after the truth. Louw's unprecedented, rational and dispassionate evaluation will perhaps encourage those who maintain that the *Freedom Charter* is sacrosanct and therefore should not be subjected to rigorous scrutiny, to revisit the logic and importance of intellectual discourse and its contribution to the intellectual nourishment of society at large.

## The Economics of Nationalisation

In Chapter 2, Professor Richard J. Grant, Professor of Finance & Economics, Lipscomb University, Nashville, Tennessee, and a former chief economist at the Chamber of Mines, discusses the economics of nationalisation from an international point of view. Why does privatisation appear to be the most likely eventual outcome of nationalisations? Why have so many countries privatised their state-owned enterprises? The idea of nationalising natural resource industries, he suggests, appears attractive because of an illusion that minerals are just lying around waiting to be picked up, which ignores the demanding and costly processes required to extract, process and market resources, and the specialised skills required in every aspect of the industry. Why is it that as state ownership expands, efficiency throughout the economy decreases? These and other questions are answered in this chapter.

## True Empowerment and Good Governance

Chapter 3, by Eustace Davie, a Director of the Free Market Foundation, puts forward alternative policies that can be utilised to address poverty and unemployment. True empowerment, he argues, could be achieved by transferring the accumulated state-owned assets, such as public enterprises and state-owned housing and land, to the people at no cost. Hernando de Soto described state-owned assets as "dead capital". Turning the assets into "live capital" in the hands of people would alleviate poverty and empower the people in both urban and rural areas. In addition, what Davie describes as "denationalising people" can be achieved by empowering the long-term unemployed by giving them the legal right to contract freely with employers of their choice in a manner that will not threaten the job security of the already employed.

## Problems with State Ownership of Enterprises

In Chapter 4, Jasson Urbach, FMF economist, provides information about the problems experienced with state ownership of enterprises in a variety of countries. Many of the problems only become glaringly obvious when state-owned enterprises are privatised, as happened when the UK privatised its state enterprises, starting in 1979. Former state monopoly industries complained that they suffered from political interference and were denied much-needed capital. Their managers did not have proper management authority and their workforces were demotivated. Industrial relations were politicised and the industries provided poor services and charged excessive prices to the public. UK privatisation was intended to solve all these problems, principally by introducing competition to improve access to capital and improve service to customers.

This chapter contains case studies of the consequences of nationalisation in Zambia, Venezuela, Bolivia, the Democratic Republic of the Congo, Chile and Ghana, as well as a report on the public-private mining partnership in Botswana.

## Nationalisation and Black Advancement

In Chapter 5, economist Vivian Abit Atud looks at the progress that black South Africans have made since 1994, and finds that economic advancement has been considerable. Freed from the strictures of apartheid, blacks have made progress in most aspects of the economy. They now dominate the public service, comprising 70 per cent of the public workforce compared to 42 per cent in 1994. Measuring ownership of the JSE by race is made complicated by the fact that shares are held by institutions such as pension and retirement funds, unit trusts, and investment companies, which in turn are owned by a diversity of races, but an analysis shows that, here also, black ownership has advanced significantly, as it has in residential housing. Through direct and indirect ownership of the JSE, blacks own a substantial share of mining companies, which they would lose if all the mines were to be nationalised.

## Rewards of Economic Freedom

Chapter 6, authored by Eustace Davie and Jasson Urbach, explains how an increase in the extent to which government takes control of economic resources, whether through taxation or nationalisation, reduces consumer sovereignty. Measuring the results of economic policies followed by the countries for which data is available over the past three decades, has allowed comparisons to be made objectively over time between those countries. This has made it possible to follow the consequences of changes in economic policies. Utilising this information, researchers are constantly discovering new correlations. The Economic Freedom of the World: 2010 Annual Report, for instance, describes research which reveals that unemployment can be reduced by increasing economic freedom, and that increased economic freedom results in fewer homicides while reduced economic freedom leads to more. In other words, there is a correlation between economic freedom and overall socio-economic progress in terms of all aspects of human development.

In conclusion, I welcome the fact that this study does not only analyse and evaluate the issue of nationalisation but also propounds very credible and pragmatic alternatives. These alternatives, if implemented, would allow the spirit of enterprise to explode and create a rising tide of economic opportunities. The display of courage required to implement some or all of the proposed policies will reveal the difference between the statesman of vision and the short-sighted politician. At the end of the day, all that is required is the political will, followed by a stroke of the statutory pen.

**Temba A. Nolutshungu**
Director
Free Market Foundation

# Nationalisation

Chapter 1

# Analysis of the ANC Youth League's Nationalisation Proposals

## Executive Summary

### Why Nationalise?

The main reason for the ANC Youth League (ANCYL) wanting to nationalise mines (followed by banks, big business generally, and much else) is its view that (a) nationalisation is required by the *Freedom Charter* and (b) the *Freedom Charter* is binding ANC policy.

### Secondary Reasons

Secondary reasons are advanced, but not accompanied by a clear causal nexus between nationalisation and intended benefits. They rely on unsubstantiated assertions regarding the expected efficacy of nationalisation, whereas economic theory and empirical evidence suggests (a) that nationalisation is likely to be ineffective or counter-productive, and (b) that there are proven alternatives.

### Objectives

Stated objectives are:

1. Implementing the *Freedom Charter*.
2. Increased fiscal capacity.
3. Better working conditions.
4. Industrialisation and job creation.
5. National sovereignty.
6. Transformation of the "accumulation path".
7. Transformation of "spatial development patterns".

## What is to be Nationalised

The ANCYL proposal is more far-reaching, ambitious and ideologically radical than has been apparent from media coverage. A great deal more than mines is to be nationalised: banks, 'strategic' industries (essentially all big business), secondary and tertiary beneficiation industries, aspects of trade (especially international trade), financial institutions, energy (electricity, petroleum, gas), property development (new towns, cities and development areas), etc.

## The Freedom Charter

**Assumptions** – The ANCYL proposal acknowledges that the relevant words ("the mineral wealth ... banks and monopoly industry shall be transferred to the people as a whole") may not mean nationalisation, and presents arguments to the effect that they do. Although the argument is elaborate and documented, it is ahistoric in that it overlooks core aspects of the historical context, particularly:

– The author of that clause in the *Freedom Charter*, Ben Turok, says it has never meant or implied nationalisation.
– The words "the people as a whole" have never been a recognised synonym for "government". The terms are, in certain contexts, juxtaposed (as in the idea that democracy is a system whereby governments are not manifestations of "the people" but are subject to "the will of the people").
– The vexed question of why, if intended, the word "nationalise" was studiously avoided in the *Freedom Charter* despite nationalisation

at the time being commonplace and popular (the policy of, *inter alia*, the national socialist apartheid regime, all other socialistic governments, most nominally capitalistic governments, and virtually all prominent intellectuals). The word "privatisation" did not exist until three decades later.

– The world's negative experience with nationalisation during subsequent decades (which, when it manifested itself, became the decisive factor that persuaded Mandela and other ANC luminaries to replace nationalisation with privatisation, albeit cautiously and in limited contexts).

**What "the people as a whole" means** – The evidence suggests that it can safely be assumed that the phrase on which the ANCYL relies does not imply nationalisation. Free market liberalism envisages ownership of wealth by the people as a whole (directly and through market institutions). Mandela said at the time that the *Freedom Charter* was not a "blueprint for a socialist state" and that dispossession of white "mining kings" and "land barons" would, instead of leading to socialism, "open … fields for … a prosperous non-European bourgeois class" where "for the first time … the non-European bourgeoisie will have the opportunity to own *in their own name* … mills and factories … and private enterprise will boom and flourish as never before" (author's emphasis). Blade Nzimande (SACP General Secretary) sees no inconsistency between the *Freedom Charter* and Minister Susan Shabangu's statement that "We are definitely not going to nationalise mines." His view is that the *Charter* and related documents (NRT, NDR, Morogoro Declaration, Green Book, etc) envisage a "capitalist system".

**Ends and means** – The *Freedom Charter*, like subsequent ANC documents (RDP, GEAR, AsgiSA, *et al*), is about means, not ends – policy objectives not specific policies – leaving questions of how best to achieve those ends to democratic contestation. In rare cases where government as a means is intended, the *Charter* says so unambiguously (as in "the aged, the orphans, the disabled and the sick shall be cared for by the state"). Such welfare happens to characterise all capitalistic economies where welfare is one of the compromises made by all economic liberals (except pure libertarians). Government welfare in capitalistic countries far exceeds what governments provide in non-market economies. This is in addition to (a) generous private charity and philanthropy, and (b) for-profit welfare, both of which are more affordable to more people in market economies. Typically, countries with more nationalisation beg for "aid" from countries with less.

## Other Objectives

**Fiscal capacity** – The ANCYL assumes that nationalisation will increase the state's "fiscal capacity" without saying why. Economist Dawie Roodt suggests that nationalisation will make things worse for the government. He points out that around 50% of mining profits already accrue to government (through direct and indirect taxes), which is achieved (a) without diverting a cent from more pressing social needs and (b) at zero risk. Conversely, owners (private and, more commonly, government) often incur losses. The ANCYL implies that nationalised shares will be bought (nationalisation, not confiscation), but provides no estimate of (a) what this will cost the fiscus, (b) which government budgets should be sacrificed to that end, (c) the cost to the country of foreign exchange diverted to acquiring foreign-owned shares, or (d) the implications for international anti-nationalisation treaties.

**Better working conditions** – There is no motivation for the idea that nationalised mines are likely to have better working conditions than private mines. The world's experience suggests the opposite, which explains, in part, why mine workers migrate (often risking and losing their lives) in only one direction: from countries with nationalised mines to ones where they are privately owned.

**Industrialise and create more jobs** – It is assumed, without explanation, that nationalisation would promote industrialisation and employment, whereas the opposite has been the world's experience. The document discusses nationalisation of resources and nationalisation of mines as if they are synonymous. Its authors appear not to know that the former has already happened and that it failed to achieve their objectives, and that there is no reason to expect the latter to succeed where the former has failed.

**Safeguard sovereignty** – There is ambivalence about foreign investment: on the one hand it is presumed to compromise sovereignty (without saying why this should be so); on the other it is assumed that nationalisation will (for unstated reasons) attract foreign investment. Since government is envisaged as being responsible for the plethora of secondary and tertiary industries suggested, it is unclear in what foreigners might be investing, or why they might want to invest in a nationalising country.

**Transform the accumulation path** – What is meant by "accumulation path", except to the extent that it appears in the context of antiquated Marxist terminology, is that South Africa is a case of "CST" (which presumably means "Colonialism of a Special Type") with "total dependence on … mining-energy-finance monopoly capital". Nationalisation will somehow "provide a viable case and space for economic diversification". In this section the ANCYL discloses its full agenda of comprehensive nationalisation (government "control and ownership of the strategic sectors of the … economy").

**Transform South Africa's unequal spatial development patterns** – That "26 locations represent the engines of the South African economy, home to 77% of all people living under minimum living level in the country, 84% of the total population and generating 95% of the national Gross Value Added (GVA)" is presumed to be self-evidently reprehensible and in need of "transformation". The suggested alternative is extreme social engineering with apartheid-like relocation of many South Africans to new cities, towns and development areas (with the people employed in countless new and unfamiliar industries), funded by government from no disclosed source.

**Patronage** – Given the overwhelming evidence against nationalisation, one of the most common questions is "why?". The official reasons are supported by little or no motivation, which raises the obvious possibility that proponents of nationalisation may have undisclosed vested interests. Protagonists of policies are usually enriched by the "empires" they create. They, along with supporters, friends and family, tend to gain substantial wealth, power, influence and status at the expense of "the people as a whole". Given the extreme degree of arbitrary power, wealth and patronage the proposal envisages, there will be patronage opportunities and other benefits not just for advocates of nationalisation, but many others, including owners of ailing mines.

Chapter 1

# Analysis of the ANC Youth League's Nationalisation Proposals

Leon Louw

NATIONALISATION

## Why Nationalise?

The primary source of the contentious proposal that mines, followed by banks and other companies, should be nationalised is an ANC Youth League (ANCYL) document entitled *Towards the transfer of mineral wealth to the ownership of the people as a whole: A perspective on nationalisation of mines* published in February 2010 (the *Basic Document*). This has to be read with the ANCYL's *Response to a Component of the ANC Discussion Document on Economic Transformation* (the *Supplemental Document*). Other ANCYL documents dealing with its nationalisation proposal do not add anything distinctive so are not included in this analysis.

It is widely and mistakenly assumed that nationalisation has been proposed to address the country's most pressing economic problems, such as poverty and unemployment. The main justification, however, is that nationalisation is the ANCYL's view that (a) it is required by the 1955 *Freedom Charter*, and (b) all provisions of the *Charter* are binding on the ANC.

The prevailing public discourse revolves around the ANCYL's call for nationalising mines, whereas what the *Basic Document* proposes is more far-reaching, ambitious and ideologically radical than has been apparent from media coverage. What is to be nationalised after mines includes banks, "monopoly" and "strategic" industries (essentially all big business), secondary and tertiary beneficiation industries, aspects of trade (especially international trade), financial institutions, energy (electricity, petroleum, gas), property development (new towns, cities and "development" areas), and more. Reminiscent of the homeland policy of old is the extensive social engineering that is envisaged, which includes resettling millions of people into currently impoverished areas that are intended to be new growth points, and the substantial increase in anti-market regulation and intervention.

This section of the study analyses the ANCYL *Basic Document* and related considerations, including whether:

1. Nationalisation really is a *Freedom Charter* imperative.
2. The supposed "nationalisation clause" is binding on the ANC or the Alliance.
3. Nationalisation, if it were indeed ANC policy at the time, should still be regarded as such.
4. ANCYL arguments are sufficiently coherent or compelling to be adopted.
5. The ANCYL *Basic Document* addresses the country's leading problems adequately or at all.
6. Nationalisation is likely to achieve stated and implied objectives.
7. Alternative policies are more likely to do so.

It is disingenuous to criticise a proposal made in good faith without suggesting alternatives. Accordingly, some alternatives are suggested or implied within the analysis of the ANCYL *Basic Document*, and more substantial constructive and concrete suggestions are covered elsewhere in this study.

The most compelling aspect of the *Basic Document* is the debatable view that the *Freedom Charter* espouses nationalisation of mines and other assets. On the other hand, the *Basic Document* includes proposals and objectives that most South Africans would consider objectionable, sometimes in the extreme, such as the mass relocation of urbanised blacks back to rural areas, especially former homelands. Some objectives appear to have no rational connection with related policies, and some would be countermanded by what is proposed. The *Basic Document* is surprisingly ahistoric despite the Marxist rhetoric in some passages. It is as if it were drafted by authors unfamiliar with the *Freedom Charter*'s historical context and subsequent history.

## The Case for Nationalisation

The ANCYL *Basic Document* suggests seven reasons for nationalisation:

1. Required by the *Freedom Charter* (ownership by "the people as a whole").
2. Increased fiscal capacity.
3. Better working conditions.
4. Industrialisation and job creation.
5. National sovereignty.
6. Transformation of the "accumulation path".
7. Transformation of unequal spatial development patterns.

The first reason dominates the *Basic Document*, whereas the rest are not just secondary, but appear in some cases to have been added as an afterthought. Other arguments for nationalisation of mines and other sectors, of course, are typically advanced in the context of other countries and times, but they are not addressed here because the ANCYL did not introduce them to the discourse.

The first forty-six of the *Basic Document*'s ninety numbered paragraphs argue for nationalising mines by virtue of the *Freedom Charter*. The next seventeen paragraphs (forty seven to sixty four) advance additional arguments, mostly too briefly for substantial analysis, and the remaining paragraphs cover "What is to be Done", "Potential Challenges", "Objectives", and the "Conclusion". Analysis of the *Freedom Charter* and the ANCYL's conceptions regarding it are therefore accorded most attention.

The ANCYL is explicit about what should happen: "*NATIONALISATION OF MINES means the democratic government's ownership and control of Mining activities, including exploration, extraction, production, processing, trading and beneficiation of Mineral Resources in South Africa.*"

## The Freedom Charter

### *ANCYL Assumptions and Perspectives*

Since the ANCYL is satisfied that (a) the *Freedom Charter* demands nationalisation, (b) the nationalisation it demands includes mines, (c) the ANC is bound by the *Freedom Charter*, and (d) nationalisation is therefore *ipso facto* ANC policy, it regards nationalisation as a settled and virtually non-debatable imperative. According to the ANCYL, "Since 1991, the ANC compels all its members to sign a declaration ... to 'abide by the aims and objectives of ... the *Freedom Charter*'" which means that "all members of the ANC currently joined the ANC to amongst other things, fulfil the principles of the *Freedom Charter*". The *Basic Document* adds that the "1994, 1997, 2002 and 2007 Constitution re-affirms the principles of the *Freedom Charter* as aims and objectives of the ANC and obliges all members to abide by the *Charter* upon joining the African National Congress".

The ANCYL *Basic Document* relies primarily on and repeats a popular belief that the following words in the *Freedom Charter* unambiguously espouse nationalisation of, *inter alia*, mines:

> "... the mineral wealth beneath the soil, the banks and monopoly industry shall be transferred to the people as a whole ..."

What mitigates against the ANCYL's interpretation, perhaps fatally, is that the words "nationalise", "nationalisation" and "mines" neither appear in the quotation nor anywhere in the *Freedom Charter.* Also, none of the ANC luminaries whose quotations the ANCYL presents as evidence supposedly supporting their interpretation, have ever claimed them to be the meaning of the phrase.

These facts alone could be regarded as settling the matter conclusively, but it would be a disservice to the ANCYL not to interrogate the meaning of this pivotal phrase more thoroughly, or not to analyse other aspects of its proposals such as for nationalisation far beyond mines, for extreme social engineering and for soviet-like central planning.

The ANCYL, having concluded, it seems erroneously, that the *Freedom Charter* calls unambiguously for the nationalisation of mines and other assets, assumes that the world's half-century of failed mine nationalisation since 1955 should have no bearing on how to interpret the *Freedom Charter* in this, the twenty first century. It ascribes to the *Charter* a questionable original meaning, on the one hand, and a static meaning unaffected by time and experience, on the other. It is assumed that ideas regarded as credible, albeit contentious, fifty years ago should remain so and be forever mandatory. No reasons are advanced for these assumptions.

There is also no acknowledgement of, or significance attached to the fact that the drafters of the *Charter* studiously avoided the word "nationalisation" despite its near-universal legitimacy and popularity at the time. The evidence presented in this analysis suggests that they did so by virtue of (a) substantial disagreement within the anti-apartheid movement on the matter, and (b) the ANC not – as the ANCYL acknowledges – regarding itself as socialistic or communistic then or since.

The extent to which the ANC and those to its left had divergent ideologies was stressed by Nelson Mandela during his speech at the relaunch of the SACP in 1990. He described the ANC as consisting of "people with different ideological views, who are united by the common perspective of national emancipation represented by the *Freedom Charter*". Making the point that the *Charter* embraced diverse perspectives within a broad opposition to racial domination. The SACP, which, unlike the ANC, was for nationalisation, he said, had "fought side by side with the ANC for the common objective of the National Liberation of people, without seeking to impose its views on our movement." He spoke of the parties having "separate perspectives" and the SACP as having "fought to uphold the character of the ANC as the Parliament of the oppressed, containing within it people with different ideological views."

Another problem in the ANCYL's *Basic Document* is that there appears to be a fundamental confusion regarding what precisely is to be nationalised. It calls, for instance, for the "mineral wealth beneath the soil" to be nationalised, despite the fact that this has already been done. It also either fails to distinguish between minerals and mines, or regards them as synonymous.

In support of the view that the relevant words espouse nationalisation by implication or inference, the *Basic Document* cites rare examples of ANC luminaries, including Mandela, endorsing the transfer of assets to "the people as a whole", but it does not mention (a) the significance of how resolutely, though not absolutely, ANC representatives, including the drafters of the *Freedom Charter*, have avoided the word "nationalisation", and (b) how rarely they mention "mines" explicitly as a target for transfer or transformation.

Would they, it should be asked, have avoided the word "nationalisation" if that was what they intended, or the word "mines" if that was what they wanted to nationalise? Why would they resort to circuitous ways of saying what they supposedly meant? More fundamentally, why should the term "the people as a whole" be presumed a synonym for government? It has been observed by many leftist critics of "state capitalism" that government ownership is not synonymous with broad-based ownership by "the people". This is one of the few points of general agreement amongst leftist and liberal intellectuals.

### *Did the ANC or Mandela Call for Nationalisation?*

Since the ANCYL's *Basic Document* and the League's leader, Julius Malema, make much of Mandela's supposed espousal of nationalisation, it is worth noting the extent to which they err factually and contextually, and the greater significance of what they omit than what they cite. It is "most egregious" according to Alistair Sparks (*Malema, Mandela and Nationalisation*, *Daily Sun*, 7 March 2010) that this has "been allowed to go unchallenged". Sparks quotes Malema as saying, "In his first public address after release … Mandela said 'Nationalisation of the mines, banks and monopoly industry is the policy of the ANC and a change or modification of our view in this regard is inconceivable'." "In truth," writes Sparks, "Mandela 'rejected nationalisation … a full two years before becoming President'. Malema's quote is 'factually wrong in the first instance, and elliptical beyond that for it omits Mandela's change of mind …'. Mandela made 'no mention of nationalisation … in his first public address'."

According to the late Anthony Sampson, Mandela's authorised biographer, he admitted to not having been aware of the world's unhappy experience with nationalisation until he had been briefed by leaders from China, Vietnam and Holland, and leading experts, especially at Davos. He had, for instance, been unaware of Zambia's nationalisation debacle.

Despite some 1960s Marxist rhetoric, which seems curiously out of place, the *Basic Document* is, as mentioned above, strikingly ahistoric. It does not attempt an explanation of why the *Freedom Charter* and ANC leaders such as Mandela refer to "the people as a whole" wherever the word "nationalisation" would have been more apposite had it been intended. Nor does it mention concerns expressed at the time by prominent ANC Africanists, liberals and luminaries such as Albert Luthuli about whether the *Freedom Charter* had socialistic undertones that could be misinterpreted. It is one of history's anomalies that it took fifty years for the words in question to be misinterpreted.

It is hard to think of anyone better placed to speak authoritatively about what the words mean than the person who drafted them, Ben Turok. He is one of the few experts to have addressed the matter directly. Turok, apart from being one of the architects of the substance and form of the *Freedom Charter*, as head of the Congress of Democrats and reputedly a communist, whilst he, like Luthuli and others, may personally favour (or have favoured) nationalisation, had this to say (*Calm down. The ANC is not about to seize mines*, *The Times*, 19 July 2009) about what the words mean:

> "… the word 'nationalisation' does not appear in the clause [which] states, 'The national wealth shall be restored to the people', and, 'The mineral wealth beneath the soil shall be transferred to the ownership of the people as a whole'. (Note: 'beneath the soil')."
>
> "What was in our minds ... was to emphasise that white economic power had usurped the historical legacy of the indigenous people whose ownership had to be restored. It was the colonial aspect that the charter sought to reverse, not private ownership of property. It has never been the intention of the ANC to create a command economy by nationalisation, either then or now."

Regardless of what the words might mean, Ben Turok says:

> "… is our mining industry a candidate for nationalisation? … mining companies are now international and can easily shift capital abroad … while Cuba and the Soviet Union were able to nationalise without compensation, our prospects of doing so would be nil, and payments would be huge … the case for nationalising the mines has yet to be made convincingly … "

### *Historical Context*

The *Freedom Charter* was written when nationalisation was such a popular concept that it was espoused not only by the "left". It was commonplace in nominally "capitalist" countries, practised by the apartheid regime and its predecessors, and endorsed by most recognised intellectuals. It was widely regarded as the only way to generate sufficient capital for large-scale projects. The word "privatise" did not even exist because there was no need for it for another three decades. Marginalised "classical liberal" intellectuals propagated "denationalisation" in obscure and largely ignored texts.

In other words, failure to use the word at a time when it was a part of popular culture and the prevailing policy of most countries, was probably deliberate. An established thesis at the time was that it was avoided in order to accommodate the wide range of philosophies and ideologies within the "broad church" of the anti-apartheid movement. The ANC went to great lengths then and throughout its existence to be the natural home for all opponents of apartheid. Its leadership actively sought support and membership of advocates of non-racial capitalism. Oliver Tambo occasionally said the ANC was for "capitalism". He, like many other ANC representatives, denied the apartheid regime's allegation that the ANC was communist or socialist.

The drafters of the *Basic Document* were selective in their quotation from the *Freedom Charter*. The quotation on which the *Basic Document* relies ("The mineral wealth beneath the soil, the banks and monopoly industry shall be transferred to the ownership of the people as a whole.") can be regarded as implying some form of nationalisation only if read out of context, especially disregarding the unambiguously capitalistic nature of what follows. The questionable assumption that belonging to "the people as a whole" is a synonym for nationalisation is rendered all the more dubious by the resounding pro-market proposition that follows, namely that "all people shall have equal rights to trade where they choose, to manufacture and to enter all trades, crafts and professions". What these words mean is, unlike those which precede them, as clear as language gets. This is an unambiguous call for enterprise, including industry, to be private and free. These words coincide with the freedom-to-trade clause (§23) in our *Bill of Rights*, according to which "Every citizen has the right to choose their trade, occupation or profession freely …". Like many others in the *Freedom Charter* and the *Bill of Rights*, what we have here is consistency with, and only with, a market economy characterised by privatisation rather than nationalisation.

Apart from observing that there was every reason to be explicit – to use the "n" word – drafters and supporters of the *Charter* did not have the knowledge of history that is available now. They did not know, for instance, that experiments with nationalisation would have ghastly consequences and virtually all countries that tried it, including those best placed to do so efficiently, such as Britain, East Germany and various Central European countries, would abandon the idea.

The extent to which things have changed is reflected in the response of a foreign academic contacted for this study who stated, "I'm surprised that anyone is still interested in nationalisation. I thought it had been committed to the trash-heap of history."

When the *Charter* was drafted, countries such as the Soviet Union had not yet shown that assets owned by government are not in any intelligible sense "owned" by the people, and that "the people" are conspicuous victims of nationalisation according to virtually every quantified criterion.

The *Charter*'s drafters did not know that the people of the Soviet Union, China, Vietnam and other formerly communist countries would lose liberty directly (through government being their primary source of employment) and indirectly (through government being their primary source of welfare). They also did not know that nationalisation would be characterised by corruption, patronage, nepotism and inefficiency. They also never knew that "the people" as consumers would have fewer choices and inferior products and services. And they never suspected the emergence of a "*nomenklatura*" with special "hard currency" shops stocking luxuries unavailable to "the people". The use of the term "hard currency" was an extraordinarily shameless admission that their own currencies and economies were inferior. Since the drafters of the *Charter* knew none of this, they can be forgiven for contemplating nationalisation as an idea to be taken seriously, and are to be complimented on not succumbing to the temptation to recommend it as formal ANC policy.

This analysis is confirmed by Ben Turok in *The Times* article dated 19 July 2009:

> "The state was everywhere seen as the primary instrument. In the UK, the Labour Party introduced … some nationalisation; Latin America nationalised many industries. … Tanzania nationalised many industries, Zambia took over the copper mines and so on. … nationalisation of major industries was a well-known phenomenon … as the ANC moved to a negotiated settlement, there was no suggestion of taking over major industry, and this continues to be the formal policy position."

### *What "the People as a Whole" Means*

Given the centrality of the *Freedom Charter* in the ANCYL's case for nationalisation, analysis of the proposal should include analysis of the ANCYL's assumptions regarding it. The ANCYL does acknowledge fleetingly that its assumption of synonymity between "ownership by the people as a whole" and "nationalisation" is debatable. It does so in a section on "*Nationalisation vs. Ownership by the people as a whole*". Given the history of (a) the nationalisation debate, (b) the *Freedom Charter*, (c) the ANC, (d) the broader anti-apartheid movement, and (e) the ensuing world's experience, the ANCYL has a heavier burden of proof than it acknowledges in this section or the balance of its documents.

The *Basic Document* includes words that follow the supposed nationalisation quotation without interrogating their significance as an aid to determining the meaning of "the people as a whole". The paragraph continues with "... all other industry and trade shall be controlled to assist the well-being of the people; all people shall have equal rights to trade where they choose, to manufacture and to enter all trades, crafts and professions".

A striking feature of these words contained in the paragraph on which the call for nationalisation hinges is either their liberalism, or, at least, their ambiguity. They are words that resonate with, and only with, pro-market liberals. The Free Market Foundation, for instance, has, for its thirty-five years of advocacy, espoused everyone enjoying (in the *Freedom Charter*'s words) "equal rights to trade where they choose, to manufacture and enter all trades, crafts and professions". Regarding control, the classical pro-market position articulated by the eminent South African academic, William Hutt, and by his protégé, Raymond Ackerman, espouses the "sovereignty of the consumer", according to which paradigm industry and trade should be controlled directly by consumers in the perpetual democracy of the free market (where every Rand spent is a vote for consumer preference). Economic liberals see free markets as power exercised continually and directly by and for "the people". In this capitalistic world view, producers and suppliers are controlled most effectively for the benefit of the people by "market forces".

The Free Market Foundation has long propagated the "big giveaway" implemented in some Central European countries as they moved away from communism. "Peoples privatisation" transfers state-owned monopoly capital directly to "the people as a whole". In those countries formerly nationalised enterprises were restored to "the people", that is to all citizens or employees, turning them into truly empowered and emancipated consumer-owners and worker-owners. Unlike nationalisation, such "ownership by the people" would be in unambiguous accord with the spirit and letter of the *Freedom Charter*, whereas ownership by government would be monopolistic ownership in the extreme, where *de facto* owners would be a tiny *cabal* of omnipotent elites.

### *Land in Context*

As with mines, banks and other industries, the ANCYL interprets what the *Freedom Charter* has to say about land as espousing nationalisation. Yet land nationalisation and dispossession in South Africa, Zimbabwe and elsewhere provides a conclusive refutation of that notion. The apartheid regime acquired land from whites and relocated, some would say herded, blacks to such nationalised land into "locations" and "bantustans". Blacks in "black" areas never owned their land – it was never transferred to them – and they were condemned to being tenants or vassals of the state on nationalised land. Notwithstanding this undebated fact, the mistaken consensus of the apartheid regime and its critics was that blacks "had" 13% of the land (which curiously included "homelands" and excluded "townships"). In truth, blacks had no land.

It is worth observing that this is precisely what has happened in Zimbabwe. The Zimbabwe government, like the apartheid regime, acquired land from white farmers and relocated blacks there in forced removals where they live on, but do not own, nationalised land. What the apartheid regime called "homeland development", the Mugabe regime calls "rural development". Differences are cosmetic and rhetorical, not substantive or intrinsic.

There may be legitimate disagreement about who should own land, but there can be no credible disagreement about the obvious fact that land owned by governments is not land owned by those who occupy or work the land. There is, accordingly, neither in the words concerned, nor in their historical context, a basis for interpreting the *Freedom Charter* as contemplating land nationalisation. Nationalisation of land owned by black people, not just in "white group areas" and "black spots" outside the homelands, but land within homelands, was, after all, the purpose of the loathsome "land acts".

### *Afrikaner Nationalism, African Nationalism and Nationalisation*

One of the most obvious reasons for African nationalists (ANC) to avoid words connoting nationalisation in the *Freedom Charter* could have been that nationalisation was the policy of Afrikaner nationalists (National Party/apartheid regime). The anti-apartheid movement would have had a natural aversion to whatever the apartheid regime espoused, and would not have wanted to appear to share its vision on such a crucial issue. Furthermore, the movement cared about the plight of labour, especially mine workers and wanted improved wages and working conditions for them. It recognised that the way to achieve this aim was by increasing rather than decreasing the demand for labour, that is, the size, resources and number of employers competing for it. Nationalisation would have the opposite effect; it would reduce competition for labour to a monopsony (a single buyer), in this case, the government, which, pending liberation, was the dreaded apartheid regime.

A single State-Owned Mining Company (SOMC) such as that proposed by the ANCYL, would be a mine labour monopsony. As such, it would be less directly accountable to voters and labour than, say, a government department or municipality. Unlike private mining companies, it would face neither pro-labour and pro-efficiency competition from other mines, nor the benefits of exacting and perspicacious investors.

Bearing these considerations in mind, and the likelihood of the Afrikaner regime remaining in power for many years, meant that the ANC was unlikely to have propagated a policy that would encourage its adversaries to convert ominous talk of nationalising mines into reality. It made more sense to envisage its constituency participating directly as share owning mine owners or indirectly as members of mine owning trusts and cooperatives.

If, as Mandela and others pointed out, there were to be any nationalisation at all, it would be a temporary measure to "smash" what was perceived to be over-concentration pending redistribution to "the people". The ANC would be more true to the tradition and values of the *Freedom Charter* and the struggle against oppression if it left existing mines in the hands of competing private owners, encouraged more private investment in and ownership of mines, endorsed and supported the impressive rate by which black participation in mine ownership is increasing, sold existing government owned mines, and redistributed the "mineral wealth beneath the soil" it nationalised a few years ago into broad-based mostly black private ownership.

The ANC's elders were aware of the violent battles of white mine workers, a powerful constituency within the regime, supported by the Communist Party, against the advantageous employment of blacks by mining companies. In the circumstances, it would have made more sense to want black ownership than government ownership. They would also have been mindful of the adverse impact on "the people" of the nationalisation by successive white governments of broadcasting, airlines, the steel industry, electricity companies, SASOL, railways, schools, chemicals, water and gas companies, and the like. They lamented the cost-raising impact on low-income communities of the *de facto* nationalisation of agricultural processing and marketing. Mindful of the extent to which the regime had already nationalised competitive private companies in "strategic sectors" and consolidated them into state-owned "monopoly industries", and the extent to which it had created state-owned mining, industrial, financial and other enterprises, the ANC is unlikely to have wanted to support the omnipresent threat of mine nationalisation.

One of the strategies adopted by private mines, perceived to be Anglo-Saxon or Jewish, to avoid nationalisation was the Afrikaner equivalent of BEE, especially the creation of an Afrikaner mining house,

Gencor, and the promotion of Afrikaner investment in mining companies through such emerging Afrikaans financial institutions as Sanlam, Santam and Volkskas. Such institutional ownership is the principal means by which black ownership of mines has been growing under the ANC. Black direct and indirect ownership of locally listed mines is already conservatively estimated at over 25 per cent, and may be as much as 50 per cent. At present rates, the goal of the *Freedom Charter*, ownership by the people as a whole, will have been reached within a generation of transition provided, paradoxically, mines are *not* nationalised. If mines are nationalised, the *Freedom Charter*'s vision of broad-based ownership by black South Africans will be defeated.

All things considered, it would have been conspicuously anomalous for the ANC to be advancing what was essentially the policy of its principal political adversary, and would destroy what it has achieved for its constituency were it to resurrect archaic and anachronistic policies now.

### *Contemporary Context*

Writing about "new faces of militancy in Cosatu", Matuma Letsoalo (*Mail & Guardian*, 20 November 2009) cites as an example Irvin Jim (NUMSA), a "hardcore communist", who "lashes out at senior ANC leaders" (including Deputy President Motlante, unionist Gwede Mantashe and Mathews Phosa) regarding their non-socialistic interpretation of the *Freedom Charter*.

He quotes Jim as saying, "I don't know what *Freedom Charter* people are reading" or "which conference of the ANC has changed it".

"The *Freedom Charter* we know says the people shall share in the country's wealth. The national wealth, the heritage of our country shall be restored to our people. The mineral wealth beneath the soil, the banks and monopoly industries shall be transferred to the hands of the people. All other industries and trade shall be transferred to assist the wellbeing of our people." He concludes, "In a country where unemployment is so high, you must tamper with the current macroeconomic policies. The government must ensure that the *Freedom Charter* is executed."

Here we see one of many examples of the ahistoric and unsubstantiated assumption that the government is the people.

### *Ex-post Dogma or Original Intent*

Since there is virtually nothing in the *Freedom Charter* that is unambiguously socialistic and much that is exclusively capitalistic, how has the myth that it is socialistic become axiomatic truth? Its tones are perhaps left-of-centre, but that does not make it socialistic or communistic, a point on which virtually all scholarly commentators agree regardless of their personal persuasions. Part of the explanation for it being presumed hard left may be that the anti-apartheid movement was regarded in some circles, especially the apartheid regime, as a radical 'left-wing' revolutionary movement. Additionally, communistic and socialistic governments provided most support for the anti-apartheid movement.

An obvious flaw in the idea that opposition to apartheid was socialistic is that it fails, *inter alia*, to reflect that apartheid was more inconsistent with classical liberalism (including free market capitalism) than all schools of socialistic, fascistic and communistic thought, from 'left-wing' democratic socialism through 'right-wing' national socialism to despotic communism. Apartheid was characterised, above all, by extreme government ownership and control of human and non-human resources, especially for black South Africans.

In its opposition to apartheid, the *Freedom Charter* can be seen as a call for extending the liberty (including capitalism) enjoyed by whites to blacks, or the subjugation of whites to the authoritarian socialism applied to blacks. Palo Jordan, one of the ANC's leading intellectuals, cites with approval the ANC's 1923 *African Bill of Rights* as a call for the "extension to blacks of the rights enjoyed by whites". It included no suggestion of "radically restructuring the economy". He adds that in the same vein the *Freedom Charter* "is not a socialist document". Even so, his view is that it "entails" nationalisation without saying what leads him to that conclusion. Whilst not specifically calling for it, the *Freedom Charter* will, he suggests, "go a long way towards removing the commanding heights from ... private ownership". In other words, the *Freedom Charter* does not itself call for this, but will contribute to what he regards as a separate and subsequent goal. Nationalisation is, as he sees it, a personal aspiration not demanded by the *Freedom Charter*.

One of the most conspicuous aspects of the *Freedom Charter* is that virtually everything in it is sufficiently ambiguous – for important historical reasons it was deliberately so – to allow for alternative ideological interpretations. Accordingly, both doctrinaire socialists and liberals can read and agree with virtually everything in it. Much of it is, for instance, self-evidently more consistent with capitalism and libertarianism than with socialism or communism. Peter Hudson (*Transformation 1*, 1986), a socialist, regards the *Freedom Charter* as "notoriously ambiguous". He agrees that it is not a socialist document. Instead it demands a "classical bourgeois democracy" (democratic capitalism). That it "invokes neither the socialisation of the means of production nor the establishment of a dictatorship of the proletariat … has never prevented it from being construed as 'socialist' or at least 'anti-capitalist'," he concludes.

A 1985 ANC article draws attention to the rare but important distinction between the *Freedom Charter* and the ANC. In it, it says "founders were radical liberals rather than socialist egalitarians" and emphasises that the ANC "is not a workers party with a socialist programme. The liberation struggle is directed against white domination …".

### *The Preamble*

The celebrated opening line of the *Freedom Charter* is that "… South Africa belongs to all who live in it … and no government can justly claim authority unless it is based on the will of all the people". At the outset this tells us two things: that South Africa should be democratic, and that what is in it should belong to those who live in it. Wealth belonging to people as opposed to governments is more consistent with democratic capitalism than any other system. Here too the notion that whatever belongs to the government belongs to its subjects is neither justified by the wording concerned nor the historical context.

The second proposition is that "… people have been robbed of their birthright to land, liberty and peace …". Land rights and liberty are central tenets of classical liberalism and democratic capitalism, and are inconsistent with socialism and communism. The call for "peace" has two possible contexts: domestic and international peace. Maintaining peace (law and order) domestically coincides with the classical liberal idea that policing and justice are amongst government's few "core" functions. To the extent that interventionistic governments divert resources from maintaining peace and security to countless non-core functions, they are less liberal. Although the maintenance of international peace can be seen in various ideological contexts, wars and colonialism are, by their nature, government rather than market activities. Convoluted "neo-colonial" theories are necessary to suggest that they can be regarded as activities undertaken by private people in free and privatised capitalistic markets. That free trade has been labelled "neo-colonial" does not detract from the fact that it entails mutually volitional parties taking advantage of their "rights and opportunities".

The *Freedom Charter*'s third idea is that "… our country will never be prosperous or free until all our people live in brotherhood enjoying equal rights and opportunities". Here again we have a statement that is more capitalistic than socialistic. Socialism and communism espouse equality of outcomes as opposed to equality of opportunities. Equal opportunities necessarily lead to inequality of condition (whatever, if anything, that might mean). More "rights and opportunities" exist in an unimposed market order of free individuals than in an imposed dirigiste order (centralised control) or regulated subjects. Not only is prosperity a core objective of market capitalism, but that there is more prosperity (by all recognised indicators) when rights and opportunities are maximised is no longer subject to informed debate.

Given the primacy of rights and opportunities instead of controls and obligations in classical liberalism, the idea of people living in "brotherhood" (especially voluntarism) is profoundly consistent with it. Socialism is associated with statism, including opposition to "unbridled" freedom and a corresponding appetite for anti-liberty control over consensual social and economic human action.

The preamble's next proposition is that "... therefore ... " South Africans of all races adopt the *Freedom Charter*, which suggests that the entire document should be interpreted in accordance with these tenets. In other words, ambiguous wording should probably be interpreted in accordance with a classical liberal paradigm.

### *"The People as a Whole" or the Government?*

The balance of the *Freedom Charter* is divided into ten sections, all of which invite the preceding interpretation. By way of example, according to the third section "national wealth ... shall be restored to the people". That assets nationalised by the apartheid regime should be "restored to the people" is a classical liberal idea. Nationalisation is ownership by government; privatisation is ownership by people. Unless the Orwellian assumption is made that the government *is* the people.

What follows in the *Basic Document* is one of the few statements from which the notion is derived that the *Freedom Charter* is socialistic. It reads: "The mineral wealth ... banks and monopoly industry shall be transferred to the ownership of the people as a whole". Apart from the obvious fact that it does not say that they should be transferred to the government (nationalised), under free market capitalism such assets are owned by ordinary people directly and through market institutions. Contrary to popularised mythology, large private sector enterprises are the subject of widely dispersed ownership by "the people as a whole" mainly through insurance policies, pension schemes, medical aids, co-operatives, trade unions, savings and so forth.

Had nationalisation been what the authors of the *Freedom Charter* had in mind, they would have said so and they would have used the word. Nationalisation was, after all, so globally popular at the time – the "n" word was an "in" word – that they would have used it at least once, and, where they did not use it, they had no reason not to recommend nationalisation unambiguously. That the word and the idea were so studiously avoided is instructive and, according to some accounts, was a deliberate means of reconciling the "broad church" of anti-apartheid activists in the struggle, including liberals.

Nationalisation and centralised control (dirigisme) were so popular and commonplace that they were widespread even in nominally capitalist countries. Modern everyday words like "privatise", "liberalise", "corporatise", "commercialise" and "public-private partnerships" (PPPs) did not exist until the 1980s. Pure liberalism had become so rare that the word for it, "libertarianism", had fallen into disuse and had to be revived when the idea became respectable again.

If these words do not imply nationalisation, what do they mean? Obvious possibilities are widespread ownership (a) of the kind achieved when shares in privatised government enterprises are transferred directly to the general public, or (b) of the kind achieved through publicly owned financial institutions such as the Public Investment Corporation (PIC). Ownership implies the right of disposal, so that people who own such assets are free to dispose of them. There is nothing in the *Freedom Charter* to suggest a prohibition on the right of disposal.

The reference to "monopoly industry" is presumed by the ultra-left to refer to large-scale private industries. However, since industries not protected, created or owned by the government are in no sense "monopolies" (sole suppliers), a more plausible interpretation would be that the term refers to the only true monopoly industries in South Africa at the time, state-owned enterprises or "parastatals". Various industries had been, and were being nationalised or considered for nationalisation, and run as patronage monopolies by white regimes at the time in such areas as mining, railways, airlines, steel, chemicals, infrastructure and the like. Since the apartheid regime was a protagonist of monopoly industry, it would have been anomalous for the *Freedom Charter* to espouse more of it. It would make more sense to call, as the Free Market Foundation has been doing for thirty five years, for such monopoly industry to be transferred to "the people as a whole" by giving or selling them shares directly or through institutions.

### *Freedom Charter Liberalism*

What of provisions in the *Freedom Charter* that do not refer specifically to ownership of mines, banks and industry? Do they, as many assume, suggest a socialistic or communistic paradigm according to which socialism or communism should be read into the provisions examined above? Much of the *Charter* is consistent only with liberal democracy and democratic capitalism. Conversely, virtually none of it is consistent only with socialism or communism. The general tenor of the *Charter* implies liberal democracy or democratic capitalism. One of the few provisions which seems to be an exception is the fascistic proposition that "the state shall recognise the right *and duty* of all to work … and draw full unemployment benefits" (author's emphasis). In a free society there should, of course, be no duty to work and unemployment benefits should be available only when strict conditions are met.

Provisions normally presumed to be socialistic regarding access to education, housing, healthcare and the like are not necessarily so. None say that there must be government provision. The *Freedom Charter* leaves open the vexed question of which system is most likely to deliver such blessings most bountifully. If governments fund delivery, they do not need to produce it. On the contrary, as with pensions, computers and roads, more desired benefits are acquired with government funding when competing private suppliers undertake production and delivery than where governments fund *and* deliver, as with electricity, education, healthcare and policing. Since government budgets tend to deliver more where governments confine themselves to being funders of last resort, nationalisation should be regarded as the enemy of the *Freedom Charter* and "the people". Would the *Charter*'s and the ANCYL's health care objectives, for instance, be met more satisfactorily if the government runs nationalised hospitals or if it provides health care insurance (funding alone) for the poor to purchase healthcare from private providers?

Even if a socialistic interpretation might have seemed appropriate at a time when there was little or no empirical evidence on which to settle the debate, recent decades have settled the matter as conclusively as social science permits. As stated above, freer economies (with less nationalisation, especially of mines, banks and industry) are characterised by superior outcomes according to all recognised criteria and published indices. It is therefore no coincidence that the world's poor flee, often risking and losing their lives, in only one direction, from less free to more free economies – always from Cuba to America, never from America to Cuba; from North to South Korea, never the reverse; from the former East Germany to West Germany; from Zimbabwe to Botswana; from Indonesia to Singapore, and so on. Market economies use police to keep people out, and non-market economies use police to keep them in. It is as if the world's destitute masses know something those who purport to care for them do not, namely, that the best place to go if you are destitute is from countries with more nationalised and controlled enterprises to ones with less.

One of the many anomalies of the public discourse on social benefits is the assumption that the desire for "houses for all" or "jobs for all" is socialistic. It is as if their critics think capitalists derive sadistic thrills from having homeless and jobless compatriots. At the time of the *Freedom Charter*, before the overwhelming evidence now at our disposal, people could be excused for assuming that the best way to provide houses and jobs would be for the government to be the primary provider. But decades of subsequent experience the world over shows that adequate and decent housing is overwhelmingly more common in market economies. In other words, the world's experience is such that deliberately ambiguous provisions in the *Freedom Charter* can now be regarded as clarified, regardless of what the dominant view might have been then.

### *Ends and Means*

That anti-market interpretations of the *Freedom Charter* have been largely unchallenged means that pro-market interpretations are likely to be met with scepticism. Yet the literal meaning of the words, and their probable meaning given their historical context, suggests that populist anti-market conceptions should be regarded as more questionable.

As with the Reconstruction and Development Programme (RDP), the *Freedom Charter* is primarily about ends, not means, about policy objectives rather than specific policies, leaving the matter of selecting preferred means to ends to democratic processes.

Amongst the few explicitly socialistic ideas in the *Freedom Charter* are that "the aged, the orphans, the disabled and the sick shall be cared for by the state". This, as it happens, is characteristic of all capitalistic countries, and is one of the compromises made by virtually all advocates of capitalism except, of course, pure libertarians. The absolute amount of care provided for such people by governments in capitalistic countries far exceeds that provided by governments in non-market economies. Greater government-funded welfare in capitalistic countries is generously supplemented by private charity and philanthropy in cash and kind almost in direct proportion to how free a country's economy is.

Many of the *Freedom Charter*'s more ambiguous provisions can go either way, such as "Rent and prices shall be lowered, food plentiful and no-one shall go hungry ...". Socialists presume this to imply government ownership and/or control. Capitalists presume it to imply price minimising free competition. They point out that prices are lowest and food most plentiful (with fewest people going hungry) when farms are privately owned, and produce is processed and distributed by freely competing industries and retailers.

### *The Freedom Charter and the National Democratic Revolution (NDR)*

In addition to the *Freedom Charter*, there is reliance on the National Democratic Revolution (NDR). Although there is not as much reliance on it by the ANCYL as the *Charter*, it cannot be ignored. As a secondary consideration, it does not call for comparable in-depth analysis.

According to Blade Nzimande, General Secretary of the Communist Party (SACP), in "*What is the National Democratic Revolution?*", the ANC does not share "all the perspectives of the NDR as articulated by the SACP". He describes the "immediate objectives of the NDR" as not being socialism, but "the liberation of blacks in general and Africans in particular, and the building of a non-racial and non-sexist society". The SACP, rather than the ANC, "had conceived the NDR merely as a stepping stone or an 'instrument' towards socialism". For the SACP, "especially since the adoption of the Native Republic Thesis of 1928 ('A struggle for a native republic as a stage towards a socialist South Africa')" the NDR was a "route to socialism".

The "perspective" of the Alliance, however, was that the NDR "was not a socialist revolution, but it was not a struggle for capitalism either", and whilst the *Freedom Charter* was "not a socialist document [it] envisaged a ... major restructuring of the capitalist system ... in favour of the overwhelming majority of our people". He regards this perspective as "strengthened" by the ANC's Morogoro Conference and the Green Book in accordance with which the government should "manage capitalist relations" within a capitalistic economy.

In other words, Nzimande sees the *Freedom Charter*, the NDR, related documents and events, and the Alliance as implying capitalism. Applied to mining, this implies privately owned non-nationalised mines within a legal framework that favours "the overwhelming majority". This is a shared perspective, not only within the Alliance, but amongst all decent people, notwithstanding substantial differences within a capitalistic paradigm regarding the ideal characteristics of the legal framework under which private mine owners operate.

Nzimande suggests that there was no inconsistency between the *Freedom Charter* and Minister of Mining, Susan Shabangu's declaration that "We are definitely not going to nationalise mines ... The ongoing debate will not change the government's policy ... It must be a concern for investors, but I want to assure them that, as government, we are not going to go down that route". This is a stronger statement than the more common response to expressions of concern, which is that nationalisation is "not government policy". This diluted response begs the question of whether it might become policy.

The commissioning of research into whether mines should be nationalised suggests, despite repeated assurances to the contrary, that the government is seriously considering nationalisation. That it is doing so may be a needless concession to the ANCYL given the probable meaning of the ambiguous wording of the relevant clause in the *Freedom Charter*, the clear meaning of the *Charter* as a whole, and mounting international evidence against nationalisation as an effective means of achieving any of the objectives articulated by the ANCYL.

Two intellectual icons of the left, Raymond Suttner and Jeremy Cronin, explained during the struggle that the *Freedom Charter* was neither socialistic nor bourgeois, and that it sought instead "to win the support of all those who oppose apartheid". It represented "an alliance of various … classes and groupings … in the struggle against racial inequality". It was concerned with the struggle against apartheid, not against capitalism. Peter Hudson, another left intellectual, laments in his 1986 *Transformation* article (cited above) that the view that "the oppressed nation needs to reappropriate from the oppressing nation" is not anti-capitalist. "The resources in question could," he argues, "be transferred into the control of a class of black capitalists and state functionaries". This, according to him, "is precisely what seems to have been envisaged by Nelson Mandela in 1956".

From all the ink that has been devoted to the discourse on what the *Freedom Charter* means, it is clear that most experts are in agreement about it neither being a socialistic document nor demanding nationalisation.

## Nationalisation *vs.* Ownership by the People as a Whole (41-44)

Under this heading, this argument is essentially an elaboration of the dominant one derived from the ANCYL's interpretation of the *Freedom Charter*. It reasserts the view that "transfer of ownership to the people as a whole" amounts to government "control and ownership of the commanding heights of the economy or nationalisation". In the six paragraphs under this heading, there is, in fact, no further argument advanced in favour of nationalisation. The most important aspect of the section is the ANCYL's acknowledgement that there is disagreement on whether "ownership by the people" is synonymous with nationalisation. Whether or not the ANCYL protests too much, or whether the matter really is as free from doubt as it suggests, the ANCYL appears to contradict itself by asserting that the matter is free from doubt, yet addresses the question as if the matter is debatable.

In support of its dogmatic interpretation, the ANCYL quotes various ANC luminaries including the ANC Secretary General in 1955, yet nothing in the quotation is obviously instructive or even relevant. None of the ANC luminaries refer specifically or by implication to the wording under consideration. The late ANC President, Nobel Laureate Albert Luthuli, is quoted as saying in 1956 that "… even amongst the so-called capitalistic countries, nationalisation of certain industries and commercial undertakings has become an accepted and established fact. Only the uninitiated and ignorant would suggest that the Union of South Africa is going to Moscow because its Railways, Broadcasting and Post Office services are nationalised". The two most instructive aspects of this quotation are, firstly, that is does not purport to be an interpretation of the wording under consideration, and secondly, that it supports the point made above that nationalisation was commonplace, even in capitalistic countries and especially in South Africa. All things considered, the Luthuli quotation should therefore be regarded as contradicting rather than supporting the ANCYL interpretation. Had nationalisation been the intention, what President Luthuli had to say suggests that the *Freedom Charter* would have said so.

The risk of the *Freedom Charter* being misinterpreted as espousing nationalisation was actually addressed at the time by Luthuli. He and his Natal ANC colleagues called on the ANC (in a 1955 resolution) to review the relevant wording. He stressed that he was not personally opposed to "limited nationalisation", but that nationalisation was not and had never been ANC policy. According to him such ambiguities and the manner in which the *Charter* had been prepared meant that it was "open to criticism" and "by no means a perfect document". His view of it was that "its motive must be understood" as representing "a deep yearning for the security and human dignity from which it springs".

Despite such efforts, the *Charter*'s ambiguous wording survived a special ANC conference in 1956 amidst claims by concerned ANC members that the conference had been "packed with non-delegates and that the *Charter* was undemocratic, and might not have reflected formally adopted ANC policy then or at any other time totally railroaded as ANC policy".

After the ANCYL's unhelpful Luthuli quotation, there is a statement attributed to Nelson Mandela in 1956 which is in sharp contrast with his espousal in the same year of ownership by a new bourgeois class of blacks. The source for the quotation in the ANCYL's *Basic Document* is unfortunately a circuitous internet link back to itself. According to the quotation, Mandela, having said that the *Freedom Charter* demands nationalisation (without explaining why, if that is the case, it did not say so), regards the essential issue as being a need for "monopolies" to be "smashed up and the national wealth of the country turned over to the people". As in the *Charter*, Mandela's demand is for ownership by "the people", not by "the government". Here too the ANCYL fails to produce an unambiguous source to the effect that what the *Freedom Charter* espouses is nationalisation.

This analysis has no pretensions to being a work of scholarship, nor does it purport to be based on a comprehensive perusal of all contemporary sources. There may well be sources suggestive of nationalisation, but it is safe to say that, if they exist, they would by now have been widely publicised and well known, and the present author would probably have encountered them during his years of reading and networking within the anti-apartheid movement.

Notwithstanding this dilemma, there is, for the authors of both ANCYL documents, "absolutely no confusion on the understanding the leadership of the ANC had on the *Freedom Charter*, and the contemporary interpretations should not confuse us".

ANC President Oliver Tambo is quoted, also with the *Basic Document* itself being its own source, as saying at the Morogoro conference that "... vast monopolies ... in the hands of Europeans only... such as the mines, the sugar and wine industry [should be] transferred to public ownership ...". An internet search did not yield these precise words. They are, if accurate, as close to an unambiguous espousal of nationalisation as there can be without actually using the "n" word. Whilst they may be an expression of Tambo's personal views, or even of official ANC policy, they do not purport to be clarification by him of what the operative words in the *Freedom Charter* mean.

The final quotation is attributed to Mandela in his "first public address after release from prison" and is refuted by Alistair Sparks above. Unlike the other quotations, this one is easily checked and, as Sparks points out,

Mandela never said during that speech that "nationalisation of the mines, banks and monopoly industry is the policy of the ANC and a change or modification … is inconceivable".

Whereas it may be true that Tambo, Sisulu, Luthuli and Mandela "could not be mistaken" regarding the meaning of words in the *Freedom Charter*, it is by no means clear that they saw it as demanding nationalisation. Yet the *Supplemental Document* denounces alternative interpretations as "totally disingenuous and dishonest, and squarely … within the liberal interpretation".

What may be more instructive than real or imagined leadership quotations in the two documents is the failure to mention quotations to the opposite effect. It may be true that ownership by "the people as a whole" has been regarded by some recent ANC leaders and intellectuals as implying nationalisation, but that was not the case when the *Charter* was fresh in the minds of ANC members and political heavyweights. Its meaning was hotly debated, not to establish what it meant, but to clarify what it did *not* mean, which was socialism and nationalisation. Mandela made it clear during 1956, in response to queries raised by concerned Africanists within the ANC, that the *Freedom Charter* was not a "blueprint for a socialist state". The dispossession of white "mining kings" and "land barons" did not, he explained, entail socialism, but would "open … fields for the development of a prosperous non-European bourgeois class". He, and his colleagues, apparently regarded the *Charter* as an essentially capitalistic document in such statements as "… for the first time … the non-European bourgeoisie will have the opportunity to own *in their own name* … mills and factories … and *private enterprise will boom and flourish as never before*" (author's emphasis).

It is true that, at times, Mandela did espouse nationalisation. Like others, he did so as an expression of his personal opinion, or maybe that of the ANC, but not as his opinion of what the words mean in the *Freedom Charter*. Nationalisation of "monopolies" (as opposed to mines specifically) was necessary, he argued, not as a socialist measure, but so that monopolies can be "smashed" and wealth "turned over to the people". In other words, the objective was never nationalisation as an end in itself, but as a means to broad-based black ownership. Accordingly, once in office with a mandate to nationalise if it wished, the ANC adopted BEE, BBBEE, AA, land restitution and related policies instead, thus being true to the *Freedom Charter*'s objective of promoting participation in ownership by "the people as a whole".

Research by economist, Vivian Atud, shows that the end of apartheid has resulted in substantial, rapid, predictable and spontaneous gains in direct and indirect ownership by blacks in all spheres of ownership and participation. Her research suggests that more black advancement is attributable to spontaneous post-apartheid market forces than government intervention. Most empowerment has been "delivered", according to her, not by hand-outs, industry charters, racial procurement preferences and the like, but by the ANC's initial adoption of market-friendly policies.

Despite their proven success, instead of celebrating and accelerating liberalisation and privatisation, the ANCYL seeks to reverse what has been achieved. These policies, despite being modest and tentative, and despite many contradictions, achieved respectable rates of economic growth, improved South Africa's ranking on indices of personal and economic freedom, and ended a generation of stagnation during apartheid's twilight years.

A glimpse of what Mandela apparently thought during his last few years in prison was gained when Winnie Mandela, after conferring with him, wrote an unqualified endorsement of the best-seller, *South Africa: The Solution,* (co-authored by Leon Louw and Frances Kendall), which called for post-apartheid "people's privatisation" of state-owned undertakings, including those nationalised by the apartheid regime.

## Why Nationalise Mines? (46-68)

This section of the *Basic Document* has sub-sections which are characterised by the "nexus problem". Most entail bald assertions of desired benefits (as defined by the ANCYL) few of which are accompanied by a suggested causal nexus between those benefits and nationalisation, or a transmission mechanism whereby nationalisation might lead to intended consequences. Virtually all outcomes can, and typically are around the world, achieved without nationalisation, in most cases without even having nationalisable minerals or mines.

### *Increase the State's Fiscal Capacity (47-52)*

The *Basic Document* asserts without substantiation (47) that "government revenue that is generated from taxes will not be able to build better lives for all South Africans". It goes on to presume that it is the government's responsibility to "deliver better services ... deal with the housing backlog, free education access, better healthcare, safety and security, employment of particularly youth" and that it cannot do so if it is not "in control of the key and strategic sectors of the South African economy". The idea that nationalisation of mines has some connection with service delivery was echoed by NUMSA's Irvin Jim according to whom "unless the government puts nationalisation at the centre of its policy, service delivery will remain a pipe dream for the poor". No explanation of what the connection might be appears in any readily available source.

The ANCYL *Basic Document* does not, for instance, explain how governments in countries that rely solely on taxes manage to perform these functions, or how countries without mineral resources do so, or why countries where markets rather than governments perform these functions generally do so more satisfactorily. The ANCYL presumes that governments rather than markets are the only means by which a country's wealth benefits its citizens. It does not, for instance, consider why the world's poorer people migrate from countries where governments bear more of these responsibilities to ones where they are left to commercial and philanthropic private initiative.

The ANCYL *Basic Document* makes much of the "case study" presented by "nationalisation of strategic minerals" in Botswana. The *Basic Document* makes no distinction between nationalisation of minerals, which has already happened in South Africa, and nationalisation of mines, which it now proposes. According to the *Basic Document*, the Botswana government increased its shareholding in a single mining company, Debswana, to 50 per cent. Since it cites the Botswana example as a model to be emulated, the question arises whether it is calling for nationalisation or some kind of public/private sector partnership (PPP).

Regardless of what precisely the ANCYL has in mind as a "model" (which is addressed inconclusively in the section on *What is to be done?* (69)), there is a bald (unsubstantiated) assumption that nationalisation will increase the state's "fiscal capacity".

No one has, as far as we could establish, provided evidence to the effect that nationalisation is likely to have net fiscal benefits. Economist Dawie Roodt estimates that approximately 50 per cent of mining profits already accrue to the South African government. In other words, by virtue of taxation, it is effectively a 50 per cent shareholder in the country's mines. But, he points out, it is a disproportionately privileged *de facto* shareholder. It participates only in profits. It does so without having invested a cent in the mines from which it derives such generous revenues. And it incurs zero risk. It shares profits but not losses; a situation investors might fantasise about, but never experience.

Whilst it is unclear, the implication of the ANCYL's discourse under *What is to be done?* implies that the state's share (whether 50 per cent or 100 per cent) will be purchased rather than confiscated. There is no calculation of whether such an investment will yield a beneficial rate of return to the fiscus. If the experience with state-owned mines, including our own Alexkor, is anything to go by, the state may be better off investing surplus capital at fixed rates of return with private banks.

Perhaps, more fundamentally and problematically, the *Basic Document* does not address the question of whether "the people" would be better off if the state's resources it wants to divert to nationalisation were allocated instead to the "housing backlog, free education access, better healthcare, safety and security, employment of particularly youth".

### *Better Working Conditions*

The addition of these words to the discussion of fiscal capacity is curious since the matter is never addressed. There is no discussion, for instance, of whether working conditions in nationalised mines are generally better than those in private mines. The world's experience seems to suggest the opposite, but since the working conditions proposition is not elaborated in the *Basic Document* or, as far as we can establish, elsewhere, there is no way of knowing why "working conditions" are added in support of nationalisation.

### *Industrialise and Create More Jobs (53-58)*

It is presumed, correctly according to the world's experience, that industrialisation creates more jobs. What makes this interesting is that it is not a matter of automatic consensus in the ultra-left, where many intellectuals and activists regard micro-enterprises, rural development and peasant farming as superior means of job creation. This section implies that, but does not explain why, nationalisation of mines would entail substantial job creation. It also repeats the confusion between "state ownership and control of mineral resources" (which is already the case) and nationalisation of mines. The *Basic Document*, like the discourse around it, fails to appreciate the profound difference between the two – it discusses them at times as if they are synonymous. It asserts without substantiation that nationalisation of *minerals* will "contribute to growth of the economy, transfer skills, education and expertise to locals and give them sustainable jobs". Since such nationalisation has already happened, it is unclear why the ANCYL neither explains nor laments the failure of nationalisation to have heralded these blessings.

Confusion regarding what precisely the ANCYL means by nationalisation is compounded by the proposition that nationalisation "will be able to attract industrial investors". The world's experience is that nationalisation discourages investors of all kinds. It is asserted that "nationalisation of mines will lead to greater local beneficiation, industrialisation, growth of the economy and jobs for the majority of our people". Neither document suggests a causal nexus for such propositions. It also, as already stated, does not explain why resourceless countries often have the world's most prosperous citizens.

Although it is not asserted explicitly, the implication of the *Basic Document* is that government owned mines will be more labour-intensive.

This, in turn, implies that they will be less technologically advanced. The obvious question that arises is how mines that are technologically backward could be more productive per worker. That would be impossible, which raises the question as to whether the jobs to be created in mines would pay less and offer inferior working conditions.

The section concerned quotes with approval a resolution from the ANC's 52nd National Conference (known as "Polokwane") to the effect that "creation of decent work opportunities [should be] the primary focus of ANC policies". This presents a potentially insoluble dilemma: how to be more labour-intensive yet have improved working conditions.

The section goes on to cite the UNDP which attributes South Africa's unemployment to "insufficiency in the rate of output growth" and "declining labour intensity". It is assumed without substantiation that nationalisation of mines would improve output growth and that declining labour intensity is a bad thing. The demand for higher wages and improved working conditions supported by the ANCYL necessarily implies declining labour intensity. Maximum labour intensity of mining would occur if all mining was done by hand. Improved working conditions and productivity occur with extremely costly, sophisticated and technology- and capital-intensive mining techniques. The ANCYL quotes the UNDP as observing that workers can be more productive, which is lamented rather than rejoiced by the ANCYL. That nationalised mines would entail substantial job creation appears to be based on faith instead of analysis.

### *Safeguard Sovereignty (59-62)*

This section suggests that the ANC compromises South Africa's sovereignty by adopting policies that attract foreign investors. It makes the generous concession that foreign direct investment should not "altogether be disallowed" but certainly implies that South Africa can prosper in economic isolation and that it can achieve prosperity for all without foreign capital, technology or expertise. In an earlier section, however, the *Basic Document* suggests that nationalised mines will somehow attract foreign direct investment (FDI). It expresses the desire for nationalised mines to be "beacons of safer working environments and better working conditions, as they will not be in the narrow pursuit of profits at the expense of community and human development". There may be more concealed than revealed in this proposition. It ignores empirical and theoretical evidence on how and why the "pursuit of profits" generally outperforms nationalisation as a means of enriching communities and promoting human development.

### *Transform the Accumulation Path (63-64)*

It is intellectually challenging to clarify the thinking in the two paragraphs (63 and 64) under this heading. Except by ideological implication, there is no definition in the text of the "accumulation path" in need of transformation. It resurrects the idea that South Africa has (or had) Colonialism of a Special Type (CST). CST is presumed to explain why South Africa was an exporter of primary mining products with "total dependence on the power of the mining-energy-finance monopoly capital". "Control and ownership of the strategic sectors" will somehow transform the economy to "provide a viable case and space for economic diversification".

What this section appears to be suggesting is that millions of private investors (directly and through institutions) in the mining companies are monopolists ("monopoly capital") and that they used colonialism to monopolise mining, energy and finance. Having monopolised mining, they wrongfully exported their produce and earned foreign exchange with which South Africa could import finished products. Mining companies compound matters for the worse, it is assumed, by mining instead of diversifying into (by implication) secondary and tertiary manufacturing.

The *Basic Document* makes it clear that it is, for the time being, espousing only nationalisation of mines and not "energy-finance". The dominant form of energy, electricity, is already obviously nationalised whereas finance is a mixture of state and private capital. "Financial institutions" such as banks and insurance companies are largely privately owned although the state, government employees, and the trade union movement are major if not controlling shareholders directly and through financial institutions.

The section starts by expressing concern about exporting primary commodities and importing finished goods and services, which, one might have expected, would lead to the conclusion (given the logic of the two documents) that the state should be nationalising manufacturing and trade in services. If it nationalises mines, what is it to do with its output? All that will have changed is that the state, instead of mining companies, will be exporting primary commodities.

The most instructive aspect of this section of the *Basic Document*, is the clarity with which the ANCYL discloses its full agenda, namely government "control and ownership of the strategic sectors of the South African economy". In other words, mining is the beginning of comprehensive nationalisation. This might explain why the *Basic Document* confuses beneficiation with mining. Its architects seem to have in mind that government will take over all big business (the "commanding heights", "monopoly capital", "strategic industries" and the like), and start businesses the ANCYL thinks ought to exist. Here again there is an inescapable harmony between what is proposed and the apartheid regime, which had corresponding ideas with different names, such as "domestication", "inward industrialisation" and "strategic industries" preferably located in artificially decentralised "growth points" and "border areas", to which millions of people would be, and were, relocated. Both entail a vision of supposedly wise and powerful central planners directing society as if it is a stage play. The picture created in the ANCYL documents is, at least for me, the resurrection of apartheid era policies and a reversal of progress achieved since then.

### *Transform South Africa's Unequal Spatial Development Patterns (56-68)*

As the *Basic Document* progresses, it becomes increasingly difficult to establish what its authors have in mind. This section starts by lamenting "the fact that '26 locations represent the engines of the South African economy, home to 77% of all people living under minimum living level in the country, 84% of the total population and generating 95% of the national Gross Value Added (GVA)'". This "fact" is presumed without explanation to be self-evidently reprehensible and in need of "transformation". It could be argued that 84% of the population having 77% of the poverty and 95% of the GVA is a case for intensifying concentration into "engines" of the economy rather than, as the *Basic Document* proposes, dispersing the population into presently poverty-stricken areas such as Limpopo (cited by the *Basic Document* as a mineral-rich area with a disproportionate "poverty rate").

There is no discussion or apparent awareness of the fact that "spatial development patterns" in developed economies are characterised by the opposite of what the *Basic Document* proposes. It starts by suggesting that economic development should be more evenly dispersed especially into poorer parts of the country, but then goes on to suggest that there should be industrial development close to mines. Minerals are where they are, and no amount of government interference or nationalisation can redistribute them more "equally". Some are in or near the wealthiest parts of the country, some in impoverished former bantustans, some under uninhabited mountains, and some are under the sea. There is no established social theory according to which there should be anything other than a mine where minerals can be mined profitably, or according to which beneficiation should occur anywhere other than where conditions (such as social, physical and economic infrastructure) are favourable. Conversely, there is a great deal of theory and experience to the effect that it is needlessly wasteful and regressive to relocate people and jobs away from where conditions are favourable to places where they are not.

Industrial Development Zones (IDZs) with minerals-centred industries should be "spread out … to localities that have high levels of unemployment and have beneath the soil, mineral resources and reserves". This "basis for sustainable development" amounts to a proposal for artificial enrichment of parts of the country that happen to have mineral deposits. The *Basic Document* asserts that mineral rich localities such as Sekhukhune "have far greater economic potential because of the mineral resources underneath the soil". Such places "should be deliberately developed, beneficiated and industrialised".

Quite how the proposals in this section are meant to achieve their stated objectives is not revealed in the *Basic Document*. It is as if government ownership of mines is a magic wand or silver bullet that would develop simultaneously Johannesburg "into a modern city", mineral rich places such as Rustenburg and Sekhukhune "into cities", "other areas and territories into economic centres", and deal with the "congestion of poverty in very few cities". It is unclear whether the objective is purposefully to congest poverty in a few cities or to disperse poverty into many cities or to "deal with" poverty by eliminating it from all cities.

This section, being the last of the reasons for nationalising mines, is the culmination of the *Basic Document*'s vision, which is not only that nationalised mines and/or nationalisation of everything big will automatically produce rather than reduce mining efficiency and its contribution to the country's wealth, but result in or coincide with extreme forms of social engineering of the kind never attempted or achieved in the world's most extreme dictatorships. The proposal envisages large-scale relocation of much of South Africa's population in accordance with the master plan of a few ruling elites and the appearance of unprecedented quantities of capital from no disclosed source.

There is no recognition of the intensely competitive nature of mining and finance, inappropriately called "monopoly" capital, compared with government ownership and control, which is the only true monopoly.

The *Basic Document* envisages the creation of new cities in remote places such as Sekhukhune, and to relocate people from "26 locations". It is a vision of social engineering and relocation of much of the country's urban population to rural development areas and new cities. This is curiously Verwoerdian. Instead of areas to which people are to be relocated being called homelands, border industries and growth points in the apartheid tradition, they are called industrial development zones.

## What is to be Done? (69-80)

Sections 69 to 80 contain specific proposals. This is primarily an analysis of the meaning of the *Freedom Charter* and the ANCYL's arguments in favour of nationalisation. Since it concludes that the primary argument based on the supposed meaning of the *Charter* is flawed, and that the ancillary arguments rely on unsubstantiated assumptions in conflict with theoretical and empirical evidence, there is no need for detailed analysis of specific proposals flowing from these. There are essentially three proposals:

1. A new "State-Owned Mining Company" (SOMC).
2. Nationalisation of mines.
3. Law reform.

The SOMC will exist in addition to and ultimately own existing state-owned mining companies and related SOEs. It will "not be run like a private business corporation whose extent of progress is solely measured through the amount of profit generated". It should be "measured as per its ability, capacity and coherent determination to create jobs, maximization of the country's gain from mineral resources, contribution to socio-economic development and assistance of communities where mining happens". There is no indication of how such amorphous performance will be measured. Like so much else in the two documents, this is inescapably reminiscent of terminology used by the apartheid regime to justify its nationalisation agenda, which, according to anti-apartheid critics, had more to do with racial and ethnic patronage, and political power.

The "Expropriation Model" proposes that "the ANC's interpretation of section 25 of the Constitution should not be narrowly legalistic, and in the process falling into the scope of counter-transformation and reactionary Constitutionalists, whose interests is to solidify the imbalances and inequalities of the past". Nationalisation "is not only in the public interest, but decisively redresses the historical injustices of dispossession, forced labour, disorganisation of indigenous people through forced migrant labour and taxation".

It is pointed out above that nationalisation *is* dispossession rather than restitution of possession, and that the *Freedom Charter* proposes "ownership by the people", not nationalisation. The failure to address this crucial distinction permeates the two documents. It is, of course, the court's interpretation of the section, and not the ANC's that matters. What redressing "taxation" means is unclear.

Here again the causal nexus problem presents itself. By what mechanism or causal nexus nationalisation "redresses the historical injustices" and advances other goals is unclear. It is at times presumed to be automatic or self-evident, and at others suggested as a consequence of it being required. The implication is that something demanded politically of a nationalised enterprise will automatically – with no goal substitution or subversion – materialise due to delivery mechanisms worked out at a later date. Such mechanisms, it seems to be assumed, will be both available and effective.

But government, before considering nationalisation (or any other measure in any context) should first (a) have clearly articulated, quantified and agreed objectives and (b) satisfy itself that chosen measures are likely to have net benefits.

The proposal is for the expropriation of "not less than 50% of the existing Mines". Since one of the objectives of nationalisation is to abandon the profit motive, this implies that owners will be left with undisclosed minority shareholdings and will find themselves obliged to apply their remaining wealth to the ANCYL's transformational agenda. Owners may be compensated for formally nationalised assets but not such *de facto* nationalisation.

Whether or to what extent there will be compensation at all is unclear. It is stated that there will not necessarily be compensation, or that it may fall short of actual value. In other words, the proposal is more radical and revolutionary than has generally been realised. It envisages the option of confiscation without compensation. Apart from violating important international treaties, this could plunge South Africa into being a pariah state. In the circumstances, to protect national security and international credibility, the government might consider issuing reassurances that the current investigation will not contemplate such an extreme measure.

Proposals for law reform imply that not all mines will be nationalised, or that they may not be nationalised completely. It is suggested that "Corporations applying for mining in South Africa should be in partnership with the State-Owned Mining Company, wherein the State owns not less than 60% of the shares and right of determination".

## What are the Potential Challenges? (81-89)

The reference to why anyone might oppose nationalisation assumes no possible motive other than "subjective undertones seeking to protect political and private interests". The more substantive and well-documented concerns about the potentially counter-productive effects of nationalisation for the ANCYL's own goals are not addressed.

Concerns about the poor performance of existing nationalised enterprises, "South African Airways (SAA), ESKOM, SABC and Denel", for instance, are not seen as problems inherently characteristic of nationalised entities, but are dismissed as "not fair because in most instances, these have failed due to sheer criminality, mismanagement and patronage which characterised most of these entities and very weak accountability systems". The suggested solution is "strong accountability systems and legislative guidelines ... buttressed by strong public accountability mechanisms" which means that "the failed cases of SAA and ESKOM should not serve as a discouragement".

If it is that simple, two alternatives present themselves, firstly, to start by applying the solution to existing "failed" nationalised entities and, secondly, to nationalise mines and the rest only when proven successful. Is it not the height of irresponsibility for government to perpetuate existing failure when the formula for success is readily available, and to run the risk of more failure until it has shown itself capable of ubiquitous success?

This section goes on to address, *inter alia*, the question of "capacity" by suggesting that existing capacity is adequate and need not change merely because of nationalisation. It presumes that ownership (and incentives implied by it) is not a performance variable: "performance of companies is not just a function of private or public ownership, but mainly a function of control". This proposition is contradicted by theory and experience.

The "lame reference to the failed State-Owned Copper Mines in countries such as Zambia" is dismissed on the grounds that it "does not apply" to South Africa's "strategic minerals".

## General Observations and Commentary

This analysis of the ANCYL's *Basic Document* concentrates on its reasons for wanting nationalisation. It does not presuppose that the ANCYL's vision or objectives should be regarded as desirable national goals. The principle concern of this study is how to address the country's biggest problems, which are poverty and unemployment. The ANCYL *Basic Document* does not specify these as priorities although *en passant* references to the problems of poverty and unemployment are sprinkled throughout. It presupposes that, when its articulated objectives are met, poverty and unemployment will have been addressed.

In the context of uncertainty in the media, as opposed to the ANCYL documents, regarding what is meant by nationalisation, Mphutlane wa Bofelo, a cultural worker, social critic and socialist, reports that ANCYL leader, Julius Malema, "has suddenly come out in the clear about what he and the ANC nationalists mean by nationalization … [he] told a press briefing that all his organization is calling for is public-private partnerships" where government has a "majority shareholding". He quotes Malema as adding that "we want the formation of a state-owned mining company … Some people call it public-private partnerships, we call it nationalization". Unlike Malema, the *Basic Document* distinguishes between creating a government owned mining company and nationalisation of mines, and recommends both. What Malema proposes is a far cry from the nationalisation of extant private mines.

*En passant*, Bofelo laments what he calls the "bourgeoisie nationalist undertones of the nationalization clause and other clauses of the *Freedom Charter*".

Having analysed the ANCYL's call for nationalisation of mines and more, there is some doubt about what, precisely, it has in mind. There are striking differences between the *Basic Document* analysed here and some of the ANCYL President's statements. After citing with disapproval Julius Malema's "lavish and opulent lifestyle as well as business interests mostly sustained by government tenders", Bofelo criticises the nationalisation idea and hints at the possibility that it may not be in good faith, that it may have more to do with creating opportunities for patronage rather than national interest. This prospect is a common response to the question from baffled observers who ask "Why?". To the extent that the two documents convey the overall impression that they are in good faith and that they are concerned with a genuine desire to have the *Freedom Charter* implemented and to redress some pressing problems, it is suggested with respect that the ANCYL give more careful consideration to what the *Freedom Charter* clearly meant and means, and examines the overwhelming evidence against nationalisation and for privatisation as a means of achieving its macro-economic objectives. A great deal of empirical evidence has become available during recent years on which policies around the world are most commonly associated with the outcomes it wants for our country.

Malema and the ANCYL appear, for instance, to be unaware of the fact that the government already effectively has a "majority shareholding" in all mines, and already exercises strict controls over all aspects of mining. It has already nationalised minerals (actually confiscated them without compensation). One of the perverse consequences has been for traditional communities and private land owners to lose what may have been their most valuable asset. Mines, on the other hand, gained easier and cheaper access to minerals in many cases. A measure intended to help dispossessed people ended up causing more dispossession. Having confiscated minerals "beneath the soil", the government sells mining rights at prices and to beneficiaries determined politically rather than by objective criteria or by means that have the kinds of benefits the ANCYL envisages. The government then taxes mining profits, incomes paid to employees and consultants, mining equipment, some mining land, energy used by mines, and diverse other aspects of mining so that it already collects the equivalent of half or more of all mining profits – no one knows the exact percentage – and it does so, as explained by Roodt (above), under extremely favourable conditions, such as not having to divert a single cent from social spending to buy mining shares, and sharing only in profits, incurring no loss or risk from losses. It could hardly be in a better position.

Paradoxically, therefore, owning mines might be an inferior option for the government for various reasons, such as the fact that, in the real world, most state-owned enterprises run at losses, even after the proverbial playing fields have been tilted heavily in their favour. They generally consume wealth rather than generate it. Based on the South African experience in other contexts and international experience with mining, a state mining company is likely to achieve precisely the opposite of what the ANCYL wants to achieve.

For the government to divert its budget from social spending, education, policing and other national welfare programmes to buy shares in mines will have corresponding adverse impacts. Dilution of the interests of investors in mines, and part-nationalisation will, as many have pointed out, drive international capital and expertise to countries that welcome them. Reduced private mining investment and reduced state revenues from existing sources are likely to more than off-set whatever revenue there might be from government shares. The government will have diverted scarce resources only to find itself earning diminishing revenues. It will have sacrificed its present bonanza of high returns on zero investment. It is indeed hard to imagine by what mechanism or process the status quo could be improved from the government's or the country's perspective.

## Additional Arguments

### *ANCYL Response to a Component of the ANC Discussion Document on Economic Transformation ("Supplemental Document")*

Unfortunately the ANCYL's rejoinder to an ANC Response to its *Basic Document* tabled at the party's 2010 National General Council (GNC) meeting in Durban is undignified, demeaning and dismissive. It describes the Response, which is clearly intended as a good faith and constructive contribution to ANC policy formulation, as relying on "rhetorical questions" and making a "lame reference to the failed State-Owned Copper Mines in countries such as Zambia", which, according to the *Supplemental Document*, had been anticipated. The supposedly rhetorical questions are rejected as "opportunistic, intransigent and against the principles that the ANC seeks to achieve".

It is true that the ANC's *Discussion Document* asks rhetorical questions. Rhetorical questions are, of course, not really questions. They are a recognised, legitimate and widely used means of making statements. The *Supplemental Document* does not explain why statements made by way of rhetorical questions should be presumed to lack substance and be unworthy of response, especially in a document called the "ANCYL Response". The absence of responses to propositions advanced by rhetorical questions means, unfortunately, that they remain, for the time being, the unanswered last word on the subject.

The Response confronts some but not all of the very real concerns raised in the *Discussion Document*. Neglected issues include the near-universal propensity of nationalised enterprises to be relatively inefficient, to be net consumers rather than producers of wealth, to be characterised by more patronage, corruption and abuse, to drain rather than enrich the fiscus, to discourage investment and job creation, and so on. The *Supplemental Document* trivialises such crucial questions and rejects them as doing little more than raising "false alarms that nationalised Mines will negatively impact … growth and investment". It regards concerns derived from real world experience and data as "simply false and neo-liberal and … an ideological myth that should be dismissed with contempt".

The strident, aggressive and largely uninformative nature of the *Supplemental Document* is unfortunately a missed opportunity to provide substantive arguments in support of nationalisation, to advance constructive debate within the ANC on a divisive matter of considerable national importance, and to fill the gaps in the ANCYL's *Basic Document* identified by the ANC's *Discussion Document*, especially the absence of (a) causal mechanisms by which promised benefits are expected to flow from proposed actions, and (b) case studies in support of claims made.

The ANC's investigation into nationalisation will hopefully demand definitive data, coherent answers and informed opinion from all who contribute to it. Since what is proposed is essentially a kind of business plan, the investigation should also demand or commission a credible and quantified cost-benefit analysis (CBA) and Regulatory Impact Assessment (RIA).

### *Malema on the Financial Crisis*

The FW de Klerk Foundation quotes the ANCYL's Julius Malema, in its critique of "Julius Malema's Call To Nationalise The Mines", as being of the view that "imperialist forces are accepting the failures of capitalism". It makes two dubious concessions, namely, that the *Freedom Charter* does in fact espouse nationalisation, and that there is indeed a "crisis of capitalism".

Given the degree to which the financial crisis is the subject of an anti-market feeding frenzy on the one hand, and bizarre conceptions of its nature and causes on the other, core aspects need to be clarified.

Firstly, it is seldom clear what anti-market fundamentalists mean by "imperialist forces". The term is generally used to connote anyone who is not anti-market. If that is what Malema has in mind, he is certainly mistaken because informed protagonists of markets regard the financial crisis as a clear example of government failure. According to this view there was no "market failure" because the underlying subprime crisis was a direct result of extreme anti-market government intervention. Instead of failing, "the market" finally triumphed over government failure by causing the government-created bubble to burst despite intensified attempts by the US government to sustain it.

Secondly, there is no "crisis of capitalism". Capitalistic economies remain, even after the "crisis", by far the wealthiest and most successful on the planet. They continued, perhaps unfortunately, throughout the crisis, to provide "aid" to poorer non-capitalistic "failed states", which continued begging capitalistic countries for hand-outs and debt relief, despite joining the misinformed chorus of voices celebrating the illusory failure of capitalism.

Thirdly, there is no significant sense in which capitalism failed. Apart from remaining by far the world's most successful system, regardless of how measured, the crisis has been a crisis in specific financial markets rather than countries or economies in general. This is clear from, *inter alia*, the fact that most capitalistic economies continued growing as if there were no crisis, and newly liberalised countries which started privatising what had previously been nationalised, such as China, India, Ghana and Mauritius, continued growing at spectacular rates.

Fourthly, companies, financial sectors and countries negatively impacted were those few which were heavily invested in US sub-prime mortgage derivatives. The sub-prime mortgage "bubble" was the deliberate anti-market creation of the US government, specifically the direct consequence of thirteen gigantic Government Sponsored Enterprises (GSEs) such as Fanny Mae, Freddie Mac and Ginnie Mae. The government encouraged reckless investment in its "toxic" mortgage derivatives – something that would never happen without government interference – by declaring derivatives to be explicitly or implicitly "government backed", and by issuing repeated assurances that, thanks to substantial regulation and money creation ("quantitative easing"), derivatives and those who held them were "sound".

Fifthly, whether there can ever be such a thing as "market failure" is doubtful, simply because "the market" does not have objectives. The market is a process, not an entity. Individuals, governments and companies fail if they do not achieve stated objectives. The reason why government failure tends to be more serious than enterprise failure, which, in turn, tends to be more serious than individual failure, is that government failure can impact the entire economy, whereas enterprise failure is confined to the enterprise's sphere of influence. The financial crisis is as severe as it is because it is a manifestation of government failure.

Lessons most appropriately learned from the crisis are (a) countries that privatise tend to be more prosperous and robust than ones that nationalise, and (b) anti-market government interference tends to be counter-productive, and (c) government failure tends to occur on an immense scale.

## Nationalisation *vs.* Privatisation

### *The Evidence*

This analysis argues that nationalisation is not a *Freedom Charter* imperative and is more probably in conflict with it, and that nationalisation is likely to be counter-productive. What are the more promising alternatives?

Firstly, the nationalisation-privatisation debate may be a false dichotomy in that ownership may not be a significant variable. It could be that other policies, such as labour, trade, fiscal, monetary or technology policies are decisive variables. It seems clear from a survey of the world's and South Africa's experience that ownership does make a significant difference.

Secondly, ownership, although important, is only one component of the package of policies necessary for national prosperity, including high rates of job creation, welfare and economic growth. There is now overwhelming evidence to the effect that market-friendly policies (or reform towards such polices) are a precondition for prosperity.

It may be true that "privatisation" has for mysterious reasons become a taboo word in South Africa despite its proven virtues, but that does not detract from the inescapable fact that being for nationalisation means being against privatisation, and *vice versa*. Suggesting that nationalisation is a bad idea amounts *ipso facto* to suggesting that privatisation is a good idea, just as suggesting that exercise is healthy is the same as saying that being sedentary is unhealthy. This discourse is far too serious for it to be subverted by irrational sensitivity about terminology.

Nedbank Chief Economist, Dennis Dykes, was not deterred by reluctance to call the opposite of nationalisation "privatisation" when describing the "excellent and extensive survey of the literature by William Megginson and Jeff Netter" (Nedcor *Guide to the Economy*, 30 August 2001). Megginson and Netter published their findings in the Journal of Economic Literature, 39, June 2001 (*State to Market: A Survey of Empirical Studies on Privatisation*). Their seminal survey showed that the empirical evidence "generally supports the theoretical arguments" for privatisation and against nationalisation. The evidence suggests that in general:

- Private firms are significantly more efficient than SOEs.
- Private firms are more efficient than partially private firms.

- Whether partially private firms offer benefits over SOEs is unclear.
- Government owned firms, where government is a passive investor, can be relatively efficient if they operate in a competitive and deregulated environment, but not as efficient as privatised companies in the same environment.
- SOEs are more efficient after they have been privatised.
- Foreign ownership of privatised entities is associated with better performance.
- Change from government to private ownership does not always improve macroeconomic performance unless (depending on the circumstances) it is accompanied by institutional reform, increased competition and a sound regulatory environment.
- Whether it is best to restructure SOEs before selling, and to sell in stages or all at once, is unclear. However, since restructuring by existing managers delays the process there is less support for this practice.

### *Fears Associated with Privatisation*

Dykes addresses "fears associated with privatisation". The most common objection to privatisation (called "restructuring" in South Africa) is the fear of job losses. The second most common objection is the fear of higher prices (to fund profits).

The expectation that jobs with be lost is, paradoxically, derived from one of the greatest virtues of privatisation, namely that privatisation (with free or relatively free competition) results in increased efficiency and productivity, which means that fewer people produce more. Stated the other way around, the fear of job losses amounts to a concession that SOEs tend to be less efficient and their employees less productive. There are various well-documented explanations, such as the positive effects of market incentives, competition, the price mechanism, the need to satisfy consumers rather than politicians and officials, and so on. As far as incentives are concerned, economic theory and reality shows that, in general, the self-interest of all concerned in the private sector is to be more efficient, whereas in government it is to be less efficient – in business a busy day is a good day; in government a busy day is a bad day.

Fortuitously the fear does not usually become reality with privatisation because the increased efficiency (improved productivity, marketing, sourcing, governance, controls, pricing, etc) anticipated by the fear usually results in sufficiently increased sales, turnover and profits to more than offset the jobs that might otherwise have been lost due to increased productivity. The fear relies on the faulty assumption that all other variables are static – static analysis and the assumption of "free lunches" is at the root of most false economics. The real world is marvellously dynamic, and one of its most splendid manifestations is the positive behaviour modification associated with privatisation versus the negative behaviour modification associated with nationalisation.

According to Dykes, the evidence shows that even if there are job losses, they are "likely to be small compared with overall gains in the economy in general". He adds that "not only is growth fostered elsewhere in the industry but also in the economy at large. This has characterised much of the move towards liberalisation over the past two decades". His conclusion is that "Social objectives, such as the extension of services to uneconomic users, are best handled overtly through direct state subsidies. This means that the cost of such activities is clearly identified and controlled … If hidden, the cost may appear bearable, but if exposed, other national priorities may take precedence".

The risk of increased prices arises only if effective competition is curtailed by, for instance, perpetuating the parastatal monopolies, subsidies, protection and other privileges associated with SOEs. The propensity to abuse "market power" is enhanced, explains Dykes, if such privileges are enjoyed by privatised entities. That privatisation should be accompanied by market liberalisation is as clear to governments as it is unappealing. The natural tendency of governments when privatising is to maximise privatisation revenues by granting anti-market privileges to private investors.

Dykes addresses the argument that privatisation may lead to worse service at higher prices. He cites the celebrated example of post-privatisation electricity blackouts in California. The most instructive thing about the fact that there is an endless mantra-like repetition of that supposed "market failure", along with a tiny lexicon of other supposed privatisation failures, is that they are exceptions proving the general rule of success. Frustrated critics are confined to citing not only rare exceptions, but doing so without regard to policy failures that explain exceptions. More significantly, what California experienced was short-lived and trivial compared with enduring "rolling blackouts" in most countries with nationalised electricity where blackouts are not newsworthy simply because they are the norm.

That aside, Dykes and Chamber of Mines Chief Economist, Roger Baxter, amongst others, point out that (in Dykes' words) "this example, as well as others, is more illustrative of the importance of getting the right regulatory and competitive framework in place. The crisis in California was caused by … capped retail prices [and] competition in the wholesale market". The predictable effect of mandated sub-economic prices, unsupported by the subsidies inefficient SOEs tend to enjoy, was increased demand without increased capacity, which "threatened distributors with bankruptcy". The Californian experience is a typical unintended consequence of "consumer protection" which, though intended to protect consumers usually harms them instead. The evidence, according to Dykes, shows that, where privatisation is implemented properly, "prices fall and service gets better". He also cites a PricewaterhouseCooper survey which points to two privatisation regulatory successes. Privatised UK telecommunications and electricity costs fell between 20% and 35% in real terms despite massive increases in capital investment.

Water privatisation in the UK is one of the rare examples of apparent privatisation failure in that it was followed by higher prices, but they "would have risen even more under public sector management given the serious deterioration in infrastructure … prior to privatisation".

Rare exceptions notwithstanding, "other cross-country studies report profitability in privatised industries rising by nearly 40%, productivity by nearly 90% and, in over 90% of cases examined, improved employee conditions".

## *South African Context*

Dykes concludes with South African examples of "restructuring" (privatisation in whole or part) documented by the Treasury, including radio stations, armaments, airports, airlines, travel, telecoms and forests. To these can be added a great deal of privatisation (including "outsourcing") by local and provincial governments, and *ad hoc* examples in virtually all government departments and agencies. Dykes laments that local privatisation has been relatively slow and bedevilled by unattainable "multiple objectives". Those he cites correspond well with the wide-ranging benefits the ANCYL hopes will flow from nationalisation.

That privatisation is more likely to achieve some ANCYL objectives does not mean that it will achieve them all, at least not to the extent desired. The degree and pace of racial transformation envisaged by the ANCYL is unlikely, for instance, to be achieved if shares in state-owned entities are sold on foreign stock exchanges. The idea that nationalisation could be a temporary bridging process between "smashing up monopolies" (as Mandela put it) and a transfer "to the ownership of the people as a whole" may call for specific forms of privatisation. Nationalised minerals could be transferred to local communities. This would be an excellent way to bring about the benefits the ANCYL want for mineral-rich yet impoverished parts of the country. They could be transferred to BBBEE companies or co-operatives, or to employees in employee share schemes, or they could be privatised into the hands of companies that meet specified BEE criteria. If the principle of "peoples privatisation" is accepted, many enticing possibilities arise.

Pointing out that such options are more consistent with the ANCYL's stated objectives than nationalisation does not imply that they should be government policy. One of the great insights of economics is the "Coase Theorem" according to which the best owners from a public interest perspective tend to be those into whose hands assets pass when they are freely exchanged in relatively unregulated markets. Vivian Atud's findings suggest that spontaneous market-driven black advancement is more expeditious and substantial than generally recognised. All things considered, the best government can do for the country, for the unemployed and the poor, for racial transformation, and for industrial efficiency appears to be privatisation and liberalisation. Fortuitously, this is also most consistent with the *Freedom Charter*.

## Conclusion

This study does not question the wisdom of the ANCYL's stated objectives. It should be noted, however, that some of them are controversial although the *Basic Document* implies that they are not. For instance, all decent people share the view that there should be "better working conditions", but not that the state's "fiscal capacity" should be increased. International experience is that countries where governments have greater "fiscal capacity" (where a greater proportion of wealth is confiscated by the state) tend to be losers as measured by virtually every one of the 100-plus published indices measuring human and environmental well-being.

The objective of nationalisation as an end in itself presupposes that ownership by government is synonymous with ownership by "the people", which, it has been argued, is flawed linguistically, historically and contextually.

The assumption that nationalised industries "create more jobs" is simultaneously contentious and contradicted by the fact that countries with less nationalisation have less unemployment. A further assumption is that private ownership compromises "sovereignty". This too is clearly contradicted by reality. Many non-sovereign countries (colonies), colonised by both capitalist and communist countries, have been characterised by nationalised industries, many manifestly sovereign countries have been and are characterised by high levels of both domestic and foreign private investment.

Whether the "accumulation path" (assuming the term has coherent meaning) should be "transformed" is also unclear. Government through diverse taxes already receives around half of all mining profits. It does so without sharing in losses and without investing a rand of capital. It is, in short, in a position owners can fantasise about, but only coercive governments can convert into reality. *More* nationalisation than that which already exists would deprive the government of indulging the ultimate investor fantasy.

At the moment, ownership of mines (and the economy generally) is being *racially* transformed by such policies as BEE, BBBEE, AA, and more substantially, by spontaneous market forces. Nationalisation would reverse extant racial transformation by transferring wealth accumulated by blacks from ownership by many into *de facto* ownership by a tiny handful of privileged "*nomenklatura*", that is, at the expense of emerging black empowerment. It is no surprise that people who envisage themselves as the commissars of nationalised assets, espouse nationalisation, but this does not detract from the fact that it would be nationalisation at the expense of direct and institutional ownership by "the people".

Chapter 2

# The Economics of Nationalisation

## Executive Summary

### What is Nationalisation?

Nationalisation, in its narrowest form, is the acquisition of ownership by government of an industry, a company, or any other type of property previously private owned.

Rather than fulfilling their intended goals, nationalised industries reduce the competitiveness not only of their own industries but also those industries that depend on their services. Nationalisation inevitably leads to privatisation as happened in the UK, Canada, the Ukraine, Greece, Chile, Mexico, Zambia, Poland, Uganda and South Africa. Politicisation that envelopes nationalised companies also affects the dealings of customers and suppliers. In particular, the labour market becomes more politicised.

### Politics and Nationalisation

The illusion that minerals are just lying in the ground waiting to be picked up is probably what makes the idea of nationalising natural resource industries politically seductive. In fact, reward from this kind of industry is elusive. It is never as easy as it looks from the outside to run a business.

Experience suggests that governments tend to direct a greater percentage of revenues towards consumption leaving a smaller proportion of capital to be reinvested for future expansion of productive capacity.

Only a small portion of the ruling faction and an even smaller portion of the electorate can benefit from state control of enterprises. Unemployment and low wage rates are an indication that there is a need for more capital, more economic flexibility, legal transparency, and improved education and skills. None of these requirements are advanced by nationalisation.

## Why Nationalisation Results in Disappointment

The successful functioning of private mining companies results in constantly increasing efficiencies, especially because they face competition from other mining companies. When competition is removed through nationalisation, the very information that allows competing private mining companies to value and allocate resources efficiently is no longer available, placing managers of monopoly state-owned enterprises at a disadvantage.

Government, due to its collective nature, cannot manage the entire mining industry as efficiently as competing private mining companies. No matter how large a private company becomes, it is not integrated into the type of politicised, collective decision-making structure that characterises government. Although a government can divide its operations into semi-autonomous enterprises, it can never match the drive and creativity of the private company it replaces.

As state ownership and control in an economy increases, the information available for the efficient management of enterprises becomes distorted and declines, as does the ability to respond to the needs of consumers. This, in turn, results in a decrease in the productive capacity of the economy and its ability to satisfy the needs of consumers.

Experience suggests that the political context of state ownership will create incentives to preserve employment in the state-owned enterprise even when productivity declines and the enterprise suffers losses. In the event of persistent losses the final solution available to government is to privatise.

Chapter 2

# The Economics of Nationalisation

Richard J. Grant



## What is Nationalisation?

Nationalisation, in its narrowest form, is the acquisition of ownership by government of an industry, a company, or any other type of property. In South Africa, examples of nationalised industries and companies include the postal service (SAPO), electricity generation (Eskom), the national airline (SAA), railway service (Transnet), weapons production (Denel), forestry services (Safcol), and some mining (Alexkor). The South African government has recently also nationalised all mineral rights.

None of these industries need be state-owned, and there are examples from around the world and in South Africa of all these services being offered by private enterprises. In many cases, these now-private industries or companies had previously been nationalised. The actual results of nationalisation never seem to live up to expectations.

Invariably, nationalised companies underperform their private-sector counterparts in terms of productivity, product quality, and profitability. In most cases, nationalised companies become net drains on the public treasury. In all cases they perform below their potential. Rather than fulfilling their intended goals, they reduce the competitiveness not only of their own industry, but also all other industries in the country that depend on their less-efficient services and must pay higher taxes to cover the subsidies.

The costs of nationalisation are present, though not always readily visible, in different industries and vary according to the particular circumstances of the companies involved. Eventually, all producers in the country, whether nationalised or not, as well as consumers and most employees are made less well-off than they would have been. If history is a guide, the political pressure that gave rise to nationalisation will eventually reverse itself. This explains the continuing popularity of privatisation programmes around the world.

## Nationalisation Leads to Privatisation

Given that privatisation is the most likely outcome of nationalisation, it is worth looking at some recent examples.

In the United Kingdom, the government privatised more than 50 firms during the years from 1979 to 1997. These firms included British Telecom, British Steel, British Coal, British Gas, British Airways, and Rolls-Royce. The privatised companies represented a range of industries including electricity generation, financial services, shipbuilding, automobile production, aerospace, water services, buses, and railroad services.

Canada privatised its national oil company in 1991, after operating it for 15 years as a crown corporation (state-owned enterprise). The government sold off its few remaining shares in 2004. Canada has privatised several other services, including retail postal services.

In the Ukraine, the Coal Industry Ministry plans to complete the privatisation of its coal producing enterprises by the end of 2014. In so doing it will liquidate its state monopoly and then drastically reduce subsidies.

Greece privatised its national air carrier Olympic Airways in 2009. It has also privatised the operations of one of the docks in Athens' large

Pireaus port. The Greek government continues to privatise with planned sales of public utilities, seaports, railways, and the leasing of airports and highways.

In 1980, Chile took action to privatise its bankrupt state-run pension system. That reform quickly demonstrated itself to be a success, which encouraged other countries, such as Argentina, Peru, and Colombia to make similar changes. Chile's recently elected president plans to privatise a portion of the national copper company, Codelco.

Between 1983 and 1991, Mexico privatised at least 218 non-financial firms in 49 different industries. This resulted in substantial gains in both productivity and profitability.

Motivated by the inefficiency and poor performance of most of its state-owned enterprises, the Zambian government began its privatisation programme in 1992. Within a decade the Zambian Privatisation Agency (now Zambia Development Agency at http://www.zpa.org.zm/) had privatised most of its state-owned mining assets, including Zambia Consolidated Copper Mines (ZCCM). Since then, copper output has increased steadily. Several hundred companies from a wide range of industries have already been privatised and the process continues.

In Poland, the government has recently privatised stakes in an oil refinery and a copper mine, and has announced plans to privatise an electric generation company and a coal mine.

In 1993, Uganda began the formal privatisation process of its 139 state-owned enterprises. This included state-owned mining interests.

In South Africa, privatisations began with Iscor in 1989. But in that same year, South Africa's only state-owned mining company, Alexkor, was created from state-owned diamond mining properties. By 2002, after many years of losses, the government was prepared to privatise at least a 51% share in Alexkor. Completion of the privatisation process was interrupted by legal proceedings on land claims by the Richtersveld community. After many years of legal uncertainty, the Richtersveld community now holds a minority interest in a portion of Alexkor's operations. This settlement serves to remedy the effects of previous governments' failure to respect property rights. Alexkor continues to be a cash drain on the current government. This fact, plus the prospect of legal certainty, should again make it a candidate for future privatisation.

The tendency of nationalised companies to underperform their private counterparts is consistent and well-recognised. But interpretation of economic history is a complex task and there are many variables to consider. To many observers, the facts might not be so obvious as to speak for themselves.

Many of the costs of nationalisation are created beyond the company's gates. It is rare that nationalisation occurs in isolation. Often, the political wave that brings the nationalisation also brings increased regulation, and these new regulations will affect other industries. The politicisation that necessarily envelops the nationalised company will also affect the dealings of customers and suppliers. In particular, the labour market will be more politicised.

## Nationalisation and the Political Agenda

Calls for the nationalisation of various industries seem to rise and fall with every other generation. It is as if the memory of what happened last time is not transmitted beyond the next generation. The temptation to nationalise natural resource industries also seems to rise when the prices of the commodities involved rise. When demand for the product is strong, it appears to be easy to run a business.

It is never as easy as it looks from the outside to run a business; and the mere avoidance of a loss during good times is not the same as best possible performance. There is also the question of how the company will perform when, as often happens, prices of the commodities produced by the nationalised industry go into decline. How well can politicised management adapt to such situations?

The political seductiveness of the idea of nationalising natural resource industries might be enhanced by the illusion that minerals are just lying there in the ground waiting to be picked up. In a sense they are, but in a more serious sense they are very elusive. To be of any use to people, minerals must be found, they must be recognised, and they must be extracted and processed. Then they must be transported and delivered to those who have uses for the minerals that would make it worthwhile to extract them.

The discovery of a mineral under one's land is not the same as determining the quantity of proved reserves. Proved reserves tend to rise and fall along with corresponding fluctuations in the mineral's price and in the costs of production. The level of economic activity in the world economy as well as the relative levels of supply affect commodity prices. Costs of production can be affected by local tax and regulatory policies, labour conditions, and political uncertainties.

Proved reserves on any particular mine property, as well as in previously unreachable locations, tend to rise as technology and know-how advance. Such technological advances are neither continuous nor inevitable. Sometimes they are serendipitous, but for the most part they result from profit-directed attention to the practice of mining.

The absence of private ownership by interested individuals weakens the link between action and profit. The inability to sell a property, or one's share in it, implies an inability to gain from the improvement of that property's value. Indeed, the implied removal of the property from the market reduces both the incentive and the ability to appraise its value.

Although it is common to speak of a nationalised property as being "owned by the people", no citizen would have the right to sell his shares in that property. This is why the value of the property ceases to play a clear role in resource allocation. Without the possibility of purchase, no individual has a clear, internalised incentive to put the property to its most productive use.

Even the "dividends" from a state-owned enterprise are not put to the same use, or subjected to the same thought, as would be dividends paid to a private individual. When a state-owned company remains profitable, the royalties and dividends received by the custodial government are directed toward the needs of the state. This makes it less likely that the capital will be redirected into new productive investments as would be the case were the dividends paid out to private investors.

Experience suggests that governments will tend to direct a greater percentage of such revenues toward consumption than would a high-net-worth private investor. This means that a lower proportion of capital will be reinvested for expansion of future productive capacity, which affects the future ability to supply more goods and services to the main beneficiaries of that investment, the consumers.

That is one of the hidden costs of nationalised industry. A government that happens to own low-cost mineral deposits will find it relatively easy to achieve an accounting profit. But that does not assure us that the enterprise is efficient, particularly if the enterprise has special protections, such as monopoly privileges in exportation.

## Underlying Problems

Observers often attribute the impetus toward nationalisation to the political needs or ambitions of its advocates. Political control over any resource, whether tax breaks, subsidies, favourable regulations, or generous pay and employment opportunities, can be used to the benefit of those who wield that control.

Such political benefits are neither generalisable nor sustainable. State control of enterprises can be used for political advantage of only a small portion of the ruling faction and an even smaller portion of the electorate. This, plus the high likelihood that the nationalised enterprise will quickly become a net drain on the treasury, helps to explain why nationalisation regularly gives way to privatisation. It contains the seeds of its own destruction.

Political leaders often see nationalisation of particular companies or industries as a means to solve such problems as unemployment, low wage rates, and perceived inequality. If we judge nationalisation by its appropriateness in achieving these goals, then it fails. Nationalised companies have often been used as a vehicle for the practice of political patronage, and this is usually quite obvious. But its benefits are limited. Although the state-owned enterprise can be used to provide employment to some politically favoured workers at above-market wages, the practice will contribute to higher unemployment and lower wages in the rest of the population. It also contributes to greater inequality amongst the people, both before the law and in their personal situations.

If unemployment and low wage rates are a problem, then, what is needed, is more capital, more economic flexibility, legal transparency, and improved education and skills. None of these is promoted by nationalisation.

## Layers of Nationalisation and the Knowledge Problem

Private ownership of property provides a public service that cannot be matched by government-owned property. The ability of a private owner to realise the benefits related to good stewardship of his property encourages greater thought and care in the employment of that property. In the course of making any exchange, whether of land, machinery, services, consumer goods, or one's labour, people discover information about the relative availability of resources and the values that other people place on those resources. This is why freedom of exchange is so important.

Government, by its very nature and the source of its purchasing power, must necessarily operate differently from a business. Collective decision processes and the powers of taxation and appropriation create a relationship to resource acquisition that is very different from the voluntary trade relationships in business. Although governments have the power to command resources, businesses are better able to elicit information on consumers' needs and have an incentive to respond quickly to those needs.

This is essential to our understanding of why nationalisation generally results in disappointment. It also helps us understand why the effects of nationalisation become worse as greater parts of an economy are nationalised, whether by direct ownership or by government regulation and control of commercial activities.

If only a small portion of an industry is nationalised, then the managers of the state-owned enterprises are able to depend, in some of their transactions, on the pricing information supplied by private enterprises. But when two or more state-owned enterprises must trade with one another, co-ordination problems become more apparent.

When the South African government nationalised mineral rights in 2002, it appropriated an entire class of property. Previously, potential owners who found reason to believe in the profit potential of a particular property could bid for the mineral rights in that property. This facilitated an orderly process for moving properties into more highly valued uses. It also gave alert individuals the incentive to invest in research, exploration, and then in production facilities. The goal is to produce useful products.

Now, mining companies cannot secure mineral rights directly, but must deal with the monopoly owner of all such rights. The general economic effect of this is to weaken the process of moving ownership of the property to those who value it most highly. It also reduces a mining company's security of tenure on a particular property: it depends on the leasing and licensing process. Further, it reduces the company's ability to plan ahead and to hold property for future use.

In the process described so far, there are still at least two parties to a transaction. But if the government owns a mining company, then the government would be negotiating with itself for mineral access. Although such negotiations would be between two ostensibly separate agents, both would be subject to government control and policy. Effectively, both sides of the transaction are politicised and the link to market information and efficiency incentives is weakened.

If all mining operations were nationalised, as mineral-rights ownership is now, then the two elements would be both horizontally and vertically integrated in South Africa. For management purposes, the operating units might continue to function with their nominally separate identities. But they would all be part of one larger company, an agency of the government. As such, they will be subject to potentially conflicting incentives that would necessarily constrain their business effectiveness.

When a private mining company purchases mineral rights, it is also vertically integrated to that extent. It is certainly possible for a private mining company to purchase multiple properties. But private companies also face competition, and they will limit the size and extent of their operations in order to maintain focus and efficiency in their deployment of company resources. No matter how large a private company becomes, it is not integrated into the type of politicised, collective decision-making structure that characterises government. Certainly it has none of the constitutional duties or coercive powers of a government.

Any organisation, as it grows larger, will experience increased management challenges as the complexity of the operation increases. The need to obtain and co-ordinate more information grows with it. Private companies have natural incentives to focus on activities in which they discover a competitive advantage. They will avoid, or depart from, lines of business to which they are less well suited. They conserve resources by selling assets that they believe they are unable to employ productively. In so doing, they naturally move those resources to higher valued uses.

When a government has nationalised companies and resources, it is less capable of managing its resources in this efficiency-improving manner. With a unified ownership model, the government would necessarily lose the sensitivity to resource availability and value that is generated naturally through decentralised business relationships. Although a government can divide its operations into semi-autonomous enterprises, it can never match the drive and creativity of the private companies that it replaces.

Private companies, in a free market, are supplied with many subtle forms of information that are not available to government-owned enterprises. Shareholders in private companies are able to show their confidence in company management by purchasing or selling shares. When purchasing shares, and raising the market value of the company, they also increase the company's ability to attract capital to its operations. This serves to direct capital to activities that are most promising in terms of value creation. It does not depend on any centralised decision-making authority.

With respect to state-owned enterprises, citizens are the ostensible shareholders. But citizens are not able to sell their shares, nor are they able to increase their holdings of such shares. There is no market for the shares of state-owned enterprises, and there is no way that a citizen can make direct use of the wealth that is implied by the ownership of such shares.

Unlike the shareholder of a private company, a citizen cannot vote directly to elect members to the board of directors of a state-owned enterprise. Citizens vote only for representatives of a more general nature, such as members of Parliament. The relationship between this vote and the operations of the state-owned enterprise is much more distant than is the relationship between a private shareholder and a privately traded company. Unlike the private shareholder, the citizen has little if any incentive to research the prospects for the state-owned enterprise. There is no way that the citizen could benefit from undertaking such work, nor is there any way that this research would result in actions that would improve the operations of the state-owned enterprise.

## Government Ownership and Control

As state ownership expands, whether horizontally or vertically, throughout the economy, efficiency decreases at an increasing rate. There is always a price to be paid for state involvement in the economy. In small quantities, the burden is commensurately easy to bear. But as state involvement grows, the burden grows at the expense of the capacity to bear it.

The productive capacity in an economy is affected not only by the level of formal state ownership, but also by the influence of state control. Implicit in ownership is the right to control the use of one's property, and to limit other people's access to it. But when this right of control is weakened, a person's right of ownership is also weakened.

A government will necessarily influence the operations of a private company whenever it imposes a tax, provides a subsidy, regulates its activities, or controls prices. All such interventions serve to some extent to reduce the effectiveness of an owner's management of his property. As is the case with state ownership, small interventions are easy to bear. But as the interventions increase, the capacity of the owners to manage their resources efficiently will be limited.

The values of assets in heavily controlled industries will tend to decline relative to those in less heavily controlled industries. Resources will tend to move toward those less heavily controlled industries where they can be employed more efficiently. Accordingly, consumers of goods and services produced in the more heavily controlled industries will experience higher prices and lower availability of those products than they would have in the absence of the controls.

As the regulations that are imposed on an industry increase, the companies in that industry will take on more of the characteristics of a state-owned enterprise. The difference is that private owners can redirect future investment into other, more promising industries. This reduces the waste of resources that might otherwise occur.

State-owned enterprises generally do not share this natural tendency to conserve resources by shifting them away from their own operations into more productive uses. Experience suggests that the political context of state ownership will create incentives to preserve employment in the state-owned enterprise even when productivity declines and the enterprise suffers losses.

When the losses are no longer politically sustainable, the response is either restructuring or privatisation.

Chapter 3

# True Empowerment and Good Governance

## Executive Summary

### TRUE EMPOWERMENT

The peaceful change that occurred in South Africa and described by many as a "miracle", was no miracle. It was consistent with the noble nature of South Africa's peoples.

Drafters of the *Freedom Charter* were not to know that in the next forty years experience would provide evidence that government ownership and control of enterprises and the means of production would not benefit the people. That in the Soviet Union, for example, the people's freedoms as employees would be curtailed and as consumers they would have to accept whatever the state industries produced and supplied; that there would be no alternative choices.

### *Giving Benefits Directly to the Poor*

The ANCYL's "plan for nationalising the mines" will not, as is contended, be for the "benefit of the people as a whole". As the ANCYL admits, nationalising the mines will not give the people a direct interest in them. On the other hand if ownership of the public enterprises, land, housing, and myriad other state-owned assets are transferred to the people, they will benefit significantly, directly and with the added benefit that the transfer of ownership will not disrupt the economy.

### *Dead Capital*

Hernando de Soto, in his books *The Other Path*[1] and *The Mystery of Capital*[2], described as "dead capital" land and housing over which people have use rights but no secure legal title. They are unable to borrow against such properties to start or capitalise businesses to earn or augment incomes. A common argument against the transfer of homes by government to poor people at no or low cost is that the recipients will be reckless, immediately sell the properties for unrealistically low prices, or mortgage and end up losing them. A study carried out in Cape Town's Langa residential area did not reveal such reckless behaviour.

### *Empowerment Potential: Transform "Dead Capital" in Housing and Land into Wealth*

A mass transfer of state-owned housing and land to the people would transform what is "dead capital" in the hands of government into real assets worth billions of rand in the hands of the poorest members of society. This empowerment initiative has fundamental general support and technical and financial problems relating to the transfer of such properties to their legal occupants are being resolved. If all goes well South Africa will experience one of the greatest poverty reduction and empowerment events in its history.

The mass transfer of state-owned housing and land to the people will alleviate poverty at a low cost to taxpayers. It will also accelerate entrepreneurship, reduce crime and benefit more urban and rural people than have been reached by any other BBBEE programme.

### *Empowerment Potential: Transform "Dead Capital" in Public Enterprises into Wealth*

If the ANCYL truly want to help the poor they should argue for the transfer to the people of ownership of assets currently in state hands, such as the public enterprises. The lives of the South African poor will change for the better if they become the owners of not only the houses they live in, but also shares in the state enterprises. That would be true empowerment.

### *Denationalise People*

There has been conflict throughout history over property in people's bodies, labour and possessions. Property rights of individuals have been hard won over many centuries, but still remain under constant threat.

Leaders of movements calling for "equity" and "equality" and the expropriation of capital from its owners are known to exempt themselves. As happened in the Soviet Union, they cannot resist a better life for themselves using the appropriated resources.

### *Labour Laws and the Rights of the Unemployed*

Daunting legal and regulatory barriers have contributed to the unemployment of 366 out of every 1,000 members of South Africa's potential workforce. The unemployed have been denied their section 22 constitutional right to "choose their occupation or profession freely" and their section 23(1) "right to fair labour practices". The unemployed and potential employers have been subjected to a form of nationalisation; they are captives of the state.

### *Government, Unions and the Unemployed*

Increased job security for the employed has had the unintended consequence of excluding more than seven million people from the labour market. If there were five million more people in the workforce today, each earning a modest R1,000 to R3,000 per month, between R5 and R15 billion per month, or R60 and R180 billion per annum, would be in the hands of the poorest families in South Africa.

### *Denationalise the Unemployed*

Dramatically reduce unemployment by allowing the unemployed to contract freely with employers. Job Seeker's Certificates should be issued to the long term unemployed to exempt them from the labour laws and give them the legal right to control their own destinities and conditions of contract.

## Good Governance

Government should adopt policies and institute actions that will, as rapidly as possible, improve the lives of the poor and unemployed, and avoid actions that will have a detrimental effect on their lives. In making policy decisions on the proposal that the mines should be nationalised, good governance demands that government weigh up long and short term aspects of its actions on the broader society.

### *Regulatory Uncertainty*

Mining companies have endured a trying minerals nationalisation episode and now face renewed uncertainty. The nation deserves to be given a stable environment that is marked by regulatory certainty in which its firms can flourish and provide the jobs, goods, and services the people expect of them.

### *South Africa's Constitutional Protections*

Mine owners and the people who work for them are entitled to the constitutional rights and freedoms enjoyed by all other members of the population. They are also entitled to equal protection of the law and to just administrative action in terms of section 33 of the Constitution. Property owners are protected by section 25 of the Constitution. The threat to change the Constitution if it proves to be an obstacle to the achievement of nationalisation of the mines displays disrespect for the rule of law and the Constitution.

1 De Soto, Hernando. *The Other Path: The Invisible Revolution in the Third World*. Harpercollins, 1989.

2 De Soto, Hernando. *The Mystery of Capital: Why Capitalism Triumphs in the West and Fails Everywhere Else*. Basic Books, 2000.

# Chapter 3

# True Empowerment and Good Governance

Eustace Davie



## True Empowerment

The peaceful change that occurred in South Africa, described by many as a "miracle", was no miracle at all. It was consistent with the noble nature of South Africa's excluded peoples, who, despite the exclusion and their resultant suffering, did not harbour a desire to reverse the mechanisms of apartheid and become new tyrants.

The only apparent suggestion of nationalisation made in the *Freedom Charter* is in the first sentence of the section quoted by the ANCYL. But, even this conclusion is debatable when it is read in the context of the time when the document was drafted.

The drafters and supporters of the *Charter* did not possess the knowledge of history that we have available to us today. The experiments with socialism and communism in the territories of the Soviet Union had not yet provided them with the evidence which shows that assets held by the state are in fact "owned" by the people in control of the state machinery and not by "the people" in general.

They, as yet, did not know that the people of the Soviet Union and other communist countries would not benefit from such circumstances. That, in fact, their freedoms would be curtailed because the state was their only employer with no other available to offer them alternative employment. That, as consumers, the citizens of such countries would have to accept only whatever the state industries produced and supplied; that there would be no alternative choices. But, that the political elite would have their own special shops stocking luxuries unavailable to the ordinary people. The drafters of the *Charter* knew nothing of these events and can be forgiven for believing, if that is what they did believe, that transferring the minerals, banks and monopoly industries to the "ownership of the people as a whole" meant state ownership and control.

### *Giving Benefits Directly to the Poor*

The ANCYL's statement regarding its "plan for nationalising the mines" contends that the purpose is the "transfer of mineral wealth beneath the soil to the ownership and benefit of the people as a whole". The problem with that statement is that later in the document the ANCYL admits that after nationalisation the mines would not be in the hands of the people: "First is the understanding that nationalisation is not a be-all and end-all of economic transformation. In other words, having nationalised key parts of the economy does not automatically mean that indeed the entire wealth is in the hands of the people and that the people will benefit from such wealth."

The ANCYL admits that nationalisation will not give the people a direct interest in the mines and they will not necessarily benefit from transfer of ownership to the state. However, assets that should and can belong to the people are those huge assets accumulated in the hands of the state by the apartheid government and held as public enterprises (Alexkor, Denel, Eskom, PBMR, SAA, SA Express, TRANSNET, SAFCOL, INFRACO), land, housing, and myriad other assets. Transferring ownership of these assets to the people can be done without disrupting the economy.

## *Dead Capital*

Hernando de Soto, in his books *The Other Path*[1] and *The Mystery of Capital*,[2] describes how poor people in developing countries are hampered by lack of capital and secure title to property. Capital (such as land and housing) over which people have use rights but to which they do not have secure legal title he calls "dead capital". Because they do not have title, the people are unable to borrow against their properties to start or capitalise businesses for purposes of earning or augmenting incomes.

Even without mortgages, homeowners with good credit records are granted bank loans on the strength of their net assets, of which their homes usually form a significant part. Concerns are raised that if the government transfers homes to the people at no cost the recipients will be reckless, that they will immediately sell them and do something else with the proceeds, or mortgage them and lose them because they are unable to meet their bond payments. The fear of reckless behaviour on the part of black homeowners, who would be the main beneficiaries of a mass transfer of state-owned housing, is totally unfounded.

A study conducted in Cape Town's Langa residential area by the Free Market Foundation and the US-based Mercatus Centre, found that the majority of the homes were owned by the residents who had bought the houses at attractively low prices when afforded the opportunity. We also found that owners were resistant to mortgaging their homes and that very few changed hands.

## *Empowerment Potential: Transform "Dead Capital" in Housing and Land into Wealth*

A mass transfer of state-owned housing and land to the people would transform what is "dead capital" in the hands of government into real assets worth billions of rand in the hands of the poorest members of society. This empowerment initiative has fundamental general support and technical and financial problems relating to the transfer of such properties to their legal occupants are being resolved. If all goes well South Africa will experience one of the greatest poverty reduction and empowerment events in its history.

The clash between traditional values and the notion of freehold title in the rural areas needs to be handled with great sensitivity. Traditionalists fear that freehold title will lead to the disintegration of rural communities with negative consequences for their cultures, languages, values and traditions. That this fear is legitimate is demonstrated by the manner in which urbanisation loosens those bonds. Innovative solutions need to be found that will allow increased freehold title without disturbing the cohesion of the communities.

The fear that community homes and land could fall into the hands of non-members could be overcome by adopting a system of title that restricts sales to other members of the community and prevents sales to outsiders. There are many examples worldwide of restrictive titling, the restrictive covenants in Houston, Texas, possibly being the most well-known. This form of title could, but would not necessarily, tend to reduce the selling price of properties but would nevertheless provide greater security and mobility to owners than no title at all. There could also be surprising outcomes such as a demand from urbanised community members for holiday and retirement residences in their home communities.

Such a mass transfer of state-owned housing and land to the people will alleviate much of the poverty in the country at a low cost to taxpayers. Other consequences would be an acceleration of entrepreneurship and a reduction in crime. Most importantly, granting secure title to everyone legally living in state-owned houses and on state-owned land, in both urban and rural areas, would reach more beneficiaries than any BBBEE programme has ever reached before.

### *Empowerment Potential: Transform "Dead Capital" in Public Enterprises into Wealth*

If the ANCYL truly want to help the poor, they should argue for real ownership; transfer ownership to the people of assets currently in state hands, such as the public enterprises. The South African government could study how the Czech Republic and other Soviet bloc countries carried out such transfers, but in doing so they would have to take into account the disadvantages suffered by those countries, which did not have developed private financial markets to facilitate the transfers. The Czech Republic issued vouchers to the people, which they could exchange for shares in public enterprises but delays in the process caused frustration. South Africa could develop a much more efficient system for getting shares into the hands of the intended beneficiaries. In the Czech Republic, unit trusts had to be developed from scratch to enable people to gain a greater spread of interests in the major public enterprises. In South Africa, it would be a simple matter to agree with its already existing and highly developed unit trust companies to carry out that function.

The lives of the South African poor will change for the better if they become the owners of not only the houses they live in, but also shares in the state enterprises. That would be true empowerment. That would make real the promises that the socialists and communists make to the people but never carry out. When they say they want to take all the productive assets and transfer them to the people, but in fact transfer them to the state, control is passed to the small clique with the political power and the people gain no benefit whatsoever.

When assets are nationalised, the people do not own them, they do not control them, and the people are in a far worse position than they would have been had the assets remained in the hands of private owners. When everything is in the hands of competing private owners, the people have many firms competing for their labour or for their business as consumers. The people have the option of working hard and smart so as to become owners and employers themselves, an option they would not have if everything was nationalised and belonged to the state and when even their jobs would be allocated to them by officials and not chosen by themselves.

No "capitalist monopolists" have ever had the massive monopoly power that socialist/communist monopoly cliques in the Soviet Union, North Korea, Cuba and other such regimes have exercised over the productive resources of their countries. And no consumers in the 20th Century have had less choice and less security of supply of goods and services than was experienced by consumers in those countries. China's communist regime passed through a period of total national ownership and monopoly control before conceding its failure. Parts of China now have greater economic freedom and more rapid economic growth than any Western country. Those policy changes have transformed the lives of millions of Chinese people.

### *Denationalise People*

There is an unfortunate tendency on the part of people with collectivist philosophies to believe that less productive, capable, prudent or fortunate people have an automatic claim on the product of the labour of others. This view is encapsulated in the phrase, "From everyone according to his ability to everyone according to his need". Such a view, if applied to a nation, borders on support for some members of society to become the slaves of others.

There has been conflict throughout history over property in people's bodies, labour and possessions. In mediaeval times, serfs of nobles and vassals of the kingdom had no self-ownership and no secure property rights. It is only in the last few hundred years that individuals in freer countries have gained a greater say over their own lives and some form of protection over their persons and property. Property rights of individuals have been hard won over many centuries, but still remain under constant threat. Communists, fascists, and national socialists are in favour of returning to such times, as demonstrated in Soviet Russia, China, Cuba, Hitler's Germany, Mussolini's Italy, and Mugabe's Zimbabwe. In every one of these countries, all decision-making was vested in the ruling clique, and the people had no power or protected rights. Today, Chavez is taking Venezuela down the same path to tyranny.

When Russian scientist, Andrei Sakharov, 1975 recipient of the Nobel Prize for physics, who with Aleksandr Solzhenitsyn and Roy Medvedev, was one of the Soviet Union's three leading dissidents, became disenchanted with socialism, he "criticised centralised economic controls. He attacked the vaunted Soviet system of free education and medical care as an 'economic illusion' based on underpaid doctors and teachers and offering 'very low' quality of services". He also "condemned the 'pernicious' effects of the hierarchical class structure in which the Party-government-intellectual elite enjoys 'open and secret privileges' such as better schools, clinics, special stores and a system of supplemental salaries in special envelopes".[3]

Leaders of movements calling for "equity" and "equality" and the expropriation of capital from its owners are known to exempt themselves from their own injunctions once they gain political power. As happened in the Soviet Union, they cannot resist using the appropriated resources that prove inadequate to provide a better life for the nation but supremely adequate to provide a luxurious living for the favoured few, including themselves. Those who historically have promised to lead the masses out of poverty have also quickly turned to force and suppression to quieten protests when their policies made matters worse for the poor instead of better.

### *Labour Laws and the Rights of the Unemployed*

According to the latest statistics from Stats SA there are a total of 7.3 million unemployed people in South Africa today (narrow definition of unemployment – 4.4 million, discouraged work seekers – 2.0 million, without the means to search for work – 0.9 million, total – 7.3 million) and the actual rate of unemployment is 36.6 per cent of the potential workforce.

An abnormally high unemployment rate of such vast proportions, with 366 people out of every 1,000 members of the potential workforce unemployed, has been created over time with the implementation of daunting legal and regulatory barriers to employment. It has been allowed to escalate by denying the unemployed their right to "choose their occupation or profession freely" as stipulated in section 22 of the Constitution and "the right to fair labour practices" as in section 23(1). In fact, denying the unemployed and their potential employers the right to enter into voluntary agreements with each other on mutually agreeable terms is a form of nationalisation; it makes them captives of the state. Prohibitions on legitimate voluntary employment agreements create and maintain poverty, instability, and volatile social conditions that can all too easily become uncontrollably destructive.

### *Government, Unions and the Unemployed*

The severe barriers to entry into the labour market are enacted so as to increase the job security of those who are employed. Simultaneously, they prevent employers (including the smallest) from employing people by mutual agreement, thus excluding more than seven million people from the labour market. Without the current legislative and regulatory barriers, there could be about five million more people in the workforce today, probably earning a minimum of a conservatively estimated R5 billion and potentially R15 billion per month. This converts to a potential R60 billion to R180 billion per annum in the hands of the poorest families in the country.

The labour unions are vehemently opposed to government making even modest changes to the labour laws and regulations to allow the jobless to find work. If people manage to find a job which pays a wage below that regulated as a "decent" wage, the labour unions are swift to accuse the employer of "exploiting" the worker. The obvious inference is that to the labour unions it is better for the worker to be unemployed and have no wage at all rather than a wage that the labour union does not consider "decent". They make these pronouncements as if their support for stringent legislation, which prevents millions of people from getting work, places them on the moral high ground. They shut their eyes to the huge and escalating human misery this situation is causing.

Union leaders obviously believe that by preventing the unemployed from accepting jobs at substantially lower wages than those earned by their members, they are protecting members' interests. They probably fear that if the dammed up demand for jobs from the seven million unemployed is released, it would exert downward pressure on the wages earned by union members. If that is their conclusion, it is what is known as a "zero-sum approach", which would suggest that the wages gained by the employment of the unemployed would bring about an equivalent reduction in the wages of union members. What they need to take into account is the tendency of firms to introduce machines to do jobs when the cost of doing so is lower than the cost of labour to do the same job. Fewer unskilled workers would be unemployed if the total cost of employing them were to be reduced, making their labour more cost-effective.

A zero-sum approach wrongly assumes that there are a fixed number of jobs available in an economy. It does not take account of the huge amount of additional production that could occur in South Africa which a reduction in labour compliance costs would bring about. According to the latest statistics from Stats SA, the typical unemployed individual is a first time job seeker, has been unemployed for longer than a year, and has not completed secondary level education. The typical potential employer of such a job seeker would be an individual, small business, or non-profit organisation, in areas of activity where they would be unlikely to compete with union members. Unions should encourage this additional employment because when young people have learned the skills necessary to compete with union members they will also be candidates for swelling the ranks of the unions. The fears of the unions are unfounded; their members are well protected from retrenchment and certainly from being retrenched and replaced by inexperienced low-cost young people.

There is tremendous scope for an increase in the demand for labour. It is crucial to recognise that there will always be employment for people whose value to the employer of their productive output is greater than the cost of employing them. The cost of complying with the labour laws is a major deterrent to the hiring of labour, especially in the hiring of people with low skills. Compliance costs are as high, if not higher, for hiring a low-skilled worker at R2,000 per month as it is for hiring a higher-skilled worker at R6,000 per month. Labour law compliance costs are therefore a serious deterrent to the hiring of low-skilled workers.

Although the labour unions might be the supporters of maintaining the *status quo* it is not the unions who are primarily responsible for the situation. Parliament and the governing party are in control of the labour laws. They are responsible for nationalising the people and preventing them from gaining employment by adopting laws that deny people the right to decide for themselves what wage and conditions of employment they find acceptable. It is therefore Parliament and the governing party that has the responsibility to denationalise jobs by removing the barriers that prevent prospective employers from hiring people.

### *Denationalise the Unemployed*

Government can be forgiven for being reluctant to take on the unions in their efforts to overcome South Africa's unemployment problems. Not only is COSATU a member of the tripartite alliance but all the unions have demonstrated that they are ready and willing to take on the government by means of robust and costly industrial action. Fortunately, there is a course of action the government can follow that should not bring about a confrontation with the unions.

There are two ways to denationalise the activities of the potential entrants into new employment contracts that could dramatically reduce unemployment in the country. The one method would be to denationalise businesses and allow them to contract freely with employees on mutually beneficial terms without government intervention. This method would attract immediate opposition from labour unions and cause friction between the partners in the tripartite alliance.

The other method would be to denationalise the unemployed and allow them to contract freely with any employer of their choice on simple, mutually beneficial terms without government intervention, with the unemployed person being the only determinant of what terms are beneficial. This second method should not attract opposition from the labour unions as they surely do not take some form of sadistic pleasure in keeping the unemployed out of the job market. As matters stand, the unemployed are nationalised assets that remain so at the pleasure of the legislature. To denationalise the unemployed in this manner, would ensure that their access to the labour market disturbs the job security of people who already have jobs as little as possible.

The simple conditions of contract could be:

- Grant every person who has been unemployed for 6 months or more a Job Seeker's Certificate that is valid for two years, allowing the certificate holder to enter into an employment contract with any employer on any terms the job seeker finds acceptable and with no limit on the number of times the job seeker can change employment during the validity period of the certificate.
- Require a written contract to be entered into on inception of employment so that the conditions of employment are clear and unambiguous.
- Make a minor change to the labour law creating the Job Seeker's Certificate, stipulating that the holder of the certificate is exempt from the provisions of the labour laws, and that the employer is similarly exempt in respect only of the holder of the certificate and no other employees.

The six month waiting period is to ensure that employers do not dismiss employees and offer to take them back when they are in possession of a Job Seeker's Certificate. A written contract will protect the holder of the certificate in the event of disputes and provide evidence to the Department of Labour that the requirements of the law have been met. Applications for certificates should be dealt with as expeditiously as possible and with a minimum of administrative requirements. Sworn affidavits should be accepted as evidence of periods of unemployment, officials having warned signatories of the penalties for providing false evidence, and steps should be taken to ensure that the process is not destroyed to the detriment of the unemployed by corrupt practices.

Once long-term unemployed people are in possession of Job Seeker's Certificates, they will discover that jobs are much easier to find because the relationship between employer and employee will be conducted free of the usual entry barriers and compliance costs. Changing jobs will also be much easier and certificate holders will not be tied to dead end or extremely low paying jobs. They will be free agents in the true sense of the word and no longer the nationalised victims of laws that were intended to manage relationships between big labour and big business and not to entangle the little person.

## Good Governance

Governments face difficult decisions in formulating economic policies. Not only do they receive conflicting advice from economists and policy analysts putting forward very different, even totally opposing solutions to economic problems, they also have to contend with sometimes ill-considered or partisan pressure from their political supporters.

Modern representative democracy has evolved in a manner that places excessive demands on politicians, leading them to promise more than they can or should undertake to deliver. Politicians wend their way through a political and policy morass that can sometimes induce them to adopt policies that are counter-productive to the interests of citizens, even when they are fully aware of the probable negative consequences. Individual career politicians set out to retain the support of party constituencies and seats in the halls of power, and these objectives gain precedence over the real interests of the general electorate.

Energies of political parties become directed at retaining or gaining control of government instead of being directed at co-operating to produce legal systems that will endure and serve the best interests of citizens. The contest between political parties deteriorates to one of "buying votes" by making the most expansive promises to electorates based on the power of government to legislate, regulate and levy taxes that burden current and future taxpayers. Even worse, some politicians seek to gain support by promising to trample on constitutions, the rule of law, and the best long-term interests of all law-abiding citizens by undertaking, if they are elected, to seize assets (with or without compensation) from one group of people (citizens and non-citizens alike) for the supposed benefit of the poor.

South Africa's government today faces critical policy challenges from within its governing party that are consistent with some of the worst occurrences in constitutional democracies. Proposals being made are that the fundamental principles of our Constitution should be disregarded and the ownership of the mines be transferred to the state. If these proposals were to be adopted by the ANC and forced through Parliament, including the abandonment of the protection of property rights contained in the Bill of Rights and implicit in the principles of the rule of law, it would herald the beginning of the end for the South African Constitution. It would threaten the purpose for which all constitutions are enacted: the protection of the people from tyrannical government. Such a development would have far-reaching consequences for the nation, not merely in the short term but for future generations.

At first, nationalising the mines might sound attractive, especially to people with low incomes who are told, with no explanation as to how this is to occur, that they will benefit if ownership of the mines is transferred to the state. The purpose of this study is to provide information to government, the media and the people of South Africa on the nationalisation of the property of private firms. It discusses the merits of the case: whether the benefits of such an act for the nation are likely to exceed its costs, especially for the poor who, according to those who support the nationalisation of the mines, are to be the chief beneficiaries. Will the people of South Africa, including the poor, agree to have their constitutional property rights protection eroded if they realise that weakened property rights could allow future governments to take the property of their children, grandchildren, and great grandchildren without compensation or with inadequate compensation?

Government needs to adopt policies and institute actions that will improve the lives, as rapidly as possible, of those members of our nation who are poor, unemployed and face a future that appears to be without any apparent hope of improvement. However, their plight should not be used as an excuse to tamper with the Constitution and the rule of law in South Africa. There are alternative and vastly superior and non-destructive policies that can be instituted to assist the poor.

In making policy decisions, good governance demands that government should examine all aspects of the impact of its actions on the broader society. In considering whether nationalisation of the mines will have positive or negative consequences for citizens, government should weigh up both short and long term consequences.

Short-term consequences of proposals such as the nationalisation of the mines include the paralysing effect they have on the sector of the economy concerned. For example, the period between the first mention of nationalisation of mineral rights and the point when the legislation, regulations and departmental procedures were put in place, was one of great uncertainty for mining companies. New developments were placed on hold and business planning was disrupted for a long time and, as a consequence, the entire economy suffered.

Long-term considerations should take into account the way in which changes to the country's legal system will necessarily affect the future functioning of not only the sector concerned, but also the entire economy. When proposals to change a country's constitution are contemplated, to make possible a currently unconstitutional government action, it is not a matter of dire concern to the affected economic sector only, but to the entire nation. Constitutions are adopted in an attempt to protect citizens from ill-considered government actions motivated by short-term political initiatives. History has shown that if citizens are not protected by sound constitutions and legal systems, they all too easily become the victims of populist tyrannies.

### *Regulatory Uncertainty*

When a radical idea is thrown into the political arena, a short-term consequence is massive uncertainty. Loose talk by a junior politician can cause much uncertainty if the government fails to quash the notion he is putting forward and reassure the nation. When such radical ideas go forward for serious discussion by the governing political party, the level of unease increases substantially and untold harm is done to the economy. For any economy to flourish, regulatory certainty is essential.

All industries in South Africa are attempting to overcome the effects of a worldwide recession. Mining companies have already endured a trying minerals nationalisation episode, and now, after a brief interval of being able to operate under moderately improved conditions, face a renewed threat and are once again hampered by a suffocating pall of uncertainty.

Government owes its citizens good governance, which includes the creation and maintenance of a regulatory and policy environment that is conducive to sound business decision-making. The nation depends on its business firms to utilise resources efficiently, make profits with which to expand their operations, employ increasing numbers of people to absorb the millions that are unemployed, and be the major source of the taxes utilised in governing the country. The nation therefore deserves to be given a stable environment that is marked by regulatory certainty in which its firms can flourish and provide the jobs, goods, and services the people expect of them.

## *South Africa's Constitutional Protections*

An important long-term consideration relating to the proposed nationalisation of the mines is that such an action would be in conflict with the Constitution. The property that is protected by the Constitution consists of not only the mines, but also the homes, motor vehicles and everything else owned by every citizen of this country. They will voluntarily be giving up the constitutional protection of their own property if they allow government to amend the Constitution so that it can take over the property of the mining companies. This will be a fatal step into the unknown. How are they to know what will be done with such unbridled power in the future, possibly with their children and grandchildren suffering the consequences? Some South Africans today are threatening disrespect for our governance and legal principles. Citizens have to hold their elected and other representatives accountable. If they do not, they will suffer in the long run.

According to the South African Constitution, members of the National Assembly, for example, must swear or affirm as follows:

> I, A.B., swear/solemnly affirm that I will be faithful to the Republic of South Africa and will obey, respect and uphold the Constitution and all other law of the Republic, and I solemnly promise to perform my functions as a member of the National Assembly to the best of my ability.

The oath of office or solemn declaration is not something that should be taken lightly by people who either hold or aspire to public office. In undertaking to respect and uphold "the Constitution and all other law of the Republic" holders of political office have affirmed, *inter alia*, to respect and uphold the first Founding Provision of the Constitution, which states that:

The Republic of South Africa is one sovereign democratic state founded on the following values:

a) Human dignity, the achievement of human equality and the advancement of human rights and freedoms. (Note: This provision is supported by section 9(1) of the Constitution, which states that "Everyone is equal before the law and has the right to equal protection of the law".)
b) Non-racialism and non-sexism.
c) Supremacy of the constitution and the rule of law.
d) Universal adult suffrage, a national common voters roll, regular elections and a multi-party system of democratic government, to ensure accountability, responsiveness and openness.

Mine owners and the people who work for them are entitled to the rights and freedoms enjoyed by all other members of the population. They are also entitled to equal protection of the law. Members of the National Assembly have given a solemn undertaking to obey, respect and uphold the Constitution and the nation would therefore expect them to refrain from a biased action such as the nationalisation of the mines. Mine owners and workers are entitled to just administrative action in terms of section 33 of the Constitution. According to sub-section (1), "Everyone has the right to administrative action that is lawful, reasonable and procedurally fair".

Owners of property in South Africa are further protected by section 25 (the Property section of the Bill of Rights). Sub-section (1) states that, "No one may be deprived of property except in terms of law of general application, and no law may permit arbitrary deprivation of property".

There is no law of general application that would allow government to deprive mine owners of their property and any attempt to do so would constitute arbitrary deprivation of property and therefore be unconstitutional.

The threat to change the Constitution if it proves to be an obstacle to the achievement of nationalisation of the mines, especially if the intention were to be to do so without full or adequate compensation, is a most disturbing aspect of the rhetoric surrounding the proposal, as it displays disrespect for the rule of law and the Constitution. A sound legal system and independent, well-functioning and impartial courts are indispensable to the achievement of high economic growth and the reduction of unemployment and poverty, which is the purported purpose of the proposed nationalisation of the mines. Weakening the property rights enshrined in the Constitution will hurt the interests of the poor in the longer term and should consequently be avoided.

1 Hernando de Soto, *The Other Path: The Invisible Revolution in the Third World*, Harpercollins, 1989.
2 Hernando de Soto, *The Mystery of Capital: Why Capitalism Triumphs in the West and Fails Everywhere Else*, Basic Books, 2000.
3 Hedrick Smith, *The Russians*, Sphere Books Limited, London, 1976.

Chapter 4

# Problems with State Ownership of Enterprises

## Executive Summary

Only when public enterprises are privatised, do the deficiencies of state ownership and government management and control become apparent. The monograph, *Privatisation: A UK Success Story*,[1] provides examples of the difficulties that were being experienced by nationalised industries in the UK.

### *Political Interference*

Political involvement in the functions of monopoly state industries at various times led either to excessively low or high prices, and, inevitably, to delays in instituting desperately needed investment programmes because the government faced a whole variety of other political priorities.

### *Higher Prices*

State monopolies, divorced from genuine customer accountability, are inclined to push prices beyond a level which customers would not otherwise accept. Between 1974 and 1979, UK domestic electricity prices rose by 2 per cent every six weeks.

### *Misdirected Investment*

Delays in decision-making, caused by having to obtain government approval, interfere with the long-term strategic planning and budgeting of large state industries providing crucial services. How does government decide between the purchase of a new destroyer for the navy, the building of a hospital, and desperately needed investment capital for a state industry?

### *Management without Authority*

Managers who are subject to political authority cannot inculcate management disciplines within their organisations. As they do not have management authority, they are not fully responsible for the activities of their state corporations.

### *Demotivated Workforce*

State corporations are frequently over-staffed; the morale of the workforce is often low with a great deal of absenteeism and staff members showing a total lack of concern regarding the interests of customers.

### *Politicised Industrial Relations*

Unions often resort to strike action in order to achieve some political objective and take advantage of periods of political uncertainty to extract the maximum benefit for their workforce.

## Objectives of Privatisation

In the UK, and elsewhere, privatisation of the state industries was carried out in order to (a) encourage competition, (b) spread ownership – share ownership by private citizens has a beneficial effect on the whole economy, (c) separate ownership from regulation – the government's role as owner conflicts with its role as regulator, (d) improve access to private capital – the quality of services delivered by former UK state-owned enterprises improved when they were able to raise capital in the private capital markets and execute their plans timeously, (e) release state assets – protecting a large part of the economy from the disciplines of the market condemns the whole economy to perpetual under-performance, (f) introduce new technology – free of political control former state enterprises make purely commercial decisions about implementing new technologies, and (g) motivate the workforce – most state-owned enterprises are over-staffed and have poorly motivated employees.

## Nationalisation Case Studies

Attempts at nationalisation reveal that whenever government involves itself with business, it unleashes a conflicting mix of social and efficiency objectives. The decision to nationalise is perplexing because, in all cases, the government receives significant revenues from the private companies without carrying any of the associated risks involved in operating a business.

The case studies below describe the difficulties experienced by governments in achieving their intended objectives:

### *Zambia*

Nationalisation of the Zambian copper mines in 1969 provides important lessons about government involvement in industry. When copper prices and production fell sharply, the nationalised copper mines became a drain on government resources instead of contributing to the government's efforts to develop the country. Returned to the private sector in 2000, copper production has doubled and the mines are once again contributing to government revenue.

### *Botswana*

Botswana's mining operations consisted from the outset of a joint initiative between the private sector and government. The operations were not nationalised. The revenue sharing agreement within a predictable regulatory and tax environment has given both parties a stake in the continuing success of the mining operations. Mineral revenue has started declining in recent years and the government of Botswana has declared that the size and structure of its public sector is not sustainable and that measures will be put in place to "right-size" the sector.

### *Venezuela*

Oil production is currently responsible for about 30 per cent of Venezuela's GDP, 50 per cent of government revenue and 80 per cent of exports. Despite high oil prices GDP per capita has not increased in real terms over the past 35 years and in the last 20 years the country changed from having relatively low inflation to having a high inflation economy with inflation peaking at about 100 per cent in 1996. Under the Chávez nationalisation regime, oil production has declined, the currency was devalued by 50 per cent in early 2010, and as a result of price controls the country is experiencing shortages of goods such as sugar and milk. According to the NGO, The Venezuelan Observatory of Violence, homicides have quadrupled during Chávez's 11 years in power, with two people murdered every hour.

### *Bolivia*

Despite its large reserves of oil and natural gas, Bolivia is among Latin America's poorest nations. GDP per capita is less than one quarter of the regional average $4,780 (measured in constant 2000 prices). Nationalisation of the oil industry first occurred in 1937. Since 1952 there has been a military coup, 12 different presidents, policies have constantly changed from nationalisation to reversals of nationalisation, generally high inflation rates reached 11,750 per cent in 1985. The last regime change occurred in December 2005 when Evo Morales was elected president. In May 2006 he decreed that all foreign-owned gas and oil companies must hand over majority control to the state-owned company. Experts warn that for Bolivia to develop its economy it needs foreign-owned companies such as Brazil's Petrobras, which accounts for roughly 20 per cent of the country's GDP and 24 per cent of its tax revenue.

### *The Democratic Republic of the Congo (DRC)*

Mining was nationalised by President Mobutu Sese Seko on 31 December 1966, forming the new mining giant Gécamines (Générale de Carrières et des Mines). Initially, the original personnel were retained but over time the employees were replaced by political cronies. Between 1989 and 2003 production declined, copper by 96 per cent, zinc by 99 per cent, and cobalt by 88 per cent. By 2009 production had fallen even further, copper to 13,367t compared to the 440,848t produced in 1989. By comparison the private company Metorex Ltd produced 25,350t of copper in 2009 and expects to increase production to 140,000t by 2012.

### *Chile*

Between 1955 and 1971, Chile nationalised all mining operations under Codelco, a single state conglomerate. Anaconda Copper Mines, a major copper producer, experienced a 66 per cent decline in production following nationalisation. In 1983, Chile reformed its mining policy and private companies started operating again. As a result Codelco's share of Chilean copper production has fallen from 75 per cent in 1990 to 32 per cent in 2009. Recently, Chilean President, Sebastián Piñera, has expressed a desire to privatise Codelco.

### *Ghana*

Ghana nationalised its mining sector in the early 1960s in order to "maximise government revenue ... and employment generation". Instead, gold production fell from 915,317 ounces in 1960 to 282,299 ounces by 1984. According to the World Bank, the decline in gold and other mining sectors included: failure to maintain the mines; lack of capital investment and skills; infrastructure deterioration; high inflation; deteriorating grade of gold ore; high absenteeism and low worker discipline; pilfering, and illegal panning and smuggling of gold and diamonds. Following the implementation of radical mine privatisation in 1993, gold production increased tenfold to 2.9 million ounces in 2009. During the same period per capita GDP increased (in 2009 dollars) from $449 to $1,571.

1 Thomas O'Malley, *Privatisation: A UK success story* (1998), Johannesburg, The Free Market Foundation

Chapter 4

# Problems with State Ownership of Enterprises

Jasson Urbach

NATIONALISATION

The problems caused by state ownership and government control are generally hidden from view because of an absence of comparative alternatives. Public enterprises tend to be operated as monopolies. Only when public enterprises are privatised do the deficiencies of state ownership and government management and control become apparent. When the United Kingdom (UK) started in 1979 to transfer its state enterprises and utilities to the private sector, the success it achieved set off a wave of similar divestment strategies in other countries.

The monograph, *Privatisation: A UK Success Story*,[1] provides examples of the difficulties that were being experienced by nationalised industries in the UK:

### *Political Interference*

After the 1970s oil crisis, the UK government instructed the British Gas Corporation to hold down the domestic price of gas, but "cheap gas undercut coal-fired electricity, adding to problems of excess capacity in the electrical and coal industries. As a result of the artificially stimulated demand, the Gas Corporation had to turn away new industrial business".[2] When economic realities forced gas prices to return to their market related level, consumers who had made the switch to gas were angry with the politicians who had intended to help them by keeping prices down because they were forced to pay higher prices on their utilities bills.

Political involvement in the functions of state industries at various times leads either to excessively low prices (when commodities are subsidised), or high prices (when governments experience budget shortfalls), and inevitably to delays in instituting desperately needed investment programmes because governments face a whole variety of other political priorities.

### *Higher Prices*

"State monopolies, divorced from genuine customer accountability, are inclined to push prices beyond a level which customers would not otherwise accept. Between 1974 and 1979, UK domestic electricity prices rose by 2 per cent every six weeks."[3] State monopolies are unable, like private industry, to take immediate advantage of opportunities for cost savings.

### *Misdirected Investment*

"Under state control, the balance sheets of all state corporations become part of the state budget. All major spending has to be approved by government."[4] Borrowing by state corporations is generally underwritten by the taxpayers and therefore is subject to government approval. The consequent delays in decision-making caused by having to obtain government approval interfere with the long-term strategic planning and budgeting of large state industries providing crucial services. In the UK, key investment programmes often had to be cancelled at the last moment because government approval was delayed or not forthcoming. A chief executive in one of the privatised UK industries, when commenting on the problem of waiting in line for budgetary funding from government, said, "How does government decide between the purchase of a new destroyer for the navy, the building of a hospital, and desperately needed investment capital for a state industry?"[5]

### Management without Authority

Managers who are subject to political authority cannot inculcate management disciplines within their organisations. Also, as they do not have management authority, they are not fully responsible for the activities of their state corporations. Some managers are highly capable and reliable, but many hold their posts because of political connections or for some other reason unrelated to their management abilities.

### Demotivated Workforce

With a captive market, as in the UK, state corporations were able to charge customers high prices, yet provide poor service. An example was the telecommunications company, which was months behind in telephone installations, yet, if customers did not pay their bills, telephones were summarily cut off. State corporations are frequently over-staffed; the morale of the workforce is often low with a great deal of absenteeism and staff members showing a total lack of concern regarding the interests of customers.

### Politicised Industrial Relations

"Under state ownership, the relations between management and workforce became an issue for high politics. Pay negotiations were conducted not on the basis of what productivity had been achieved, but what the unions thought the government could afford."[6] Unions often resort to strike action in order to achieve some political objective and take advantage of periods of political uncertainty to extract the maximum benefit for their workforce.

## Objectives of Privatisation

In the UK, and elsewhere, privatisation of the state industries was carried out in order to:

### *Encourage Competition*

Competition is the only discipline that compels firms to provide competitive goods and services to consumers, keeps prices in check, improves productivity and innovation, and ensures that resources are put to their most productive uses.

### *Spread Ownership*

State ownership, supposedly, means that industrial or other assets are "held in trust" for a country's citizens and managed on their behalf for their benefit by the relevant state entity. In practice, as in the UK, citizens get a pretty poor deal. As taxpayers, they, in fact, subsidise inefficiency and, as workers, they are largely ignored and faced with inflationary price increases.

In contrast, when share ownership is extended to private citizens, it has a beneficial effect on the whole economy because the individuals holding shares usually understand that private industry needs to be run profitably in order to sustain growth.

### *Separate Ownership from Regulation*

As owner of state-owned enterprises, the UK government "was most keen to extract the maximum return from its holding, or to limit the amount of investment it had to fund".[7] When the state owns enterprises, the government's role as owner conflicts with its role as regulator. As a result of such conflict, the UK government tended to concentrate on the management of state enterprises at the expense of its primary duty of assuring good governance and equality before the law.

### *Improve Access to Private Capital*

Government oversight over borrowing by state-owned enterprises has a detrimental effect on their ability to plan for the future. Important factors responsible for the improvement in the quality of services delivered by former UK state-owned enterprises was their new-found ability to plan, raise capital in the private capital markets, and execute their plans timeously. When it comes to the complexities of providing capital, government ownership of industries and service providers makes least sense. It is impossible for governments, when dealing with their budget and loan commitments, to arrive at a purely commercial decision on providing capital and guarantees for state-owned enterprises. There are too many non-commercial considerations that impact on such funding decisions. This fatal flaw in government ownership of enterprises is probably the primary reason why privatisation occurs on such a wide scale.

### *Release State Assets*

History shows that "the state" has never been good at managing a nation's assets. To "protect" a large part of the economy from the disciplines of the market, condemns the whole economy to perpetual under-performance. Taxpayers' resources get tied up in enterprises that have little incentive to improve their efficiency. Often, taxpayers are forced to pick up the tab for losses that result from poor management or market developments for which inadequate preparation has been made.

The massive proceeds received from the sale of privatised UK enterprises enabled the UK Treasury to reduce government debt. This lessened the burden on taxpayers considerably as they no longer were required to subsidise loss-making state-owned enterprises. Taxpayers benefited as well because after privatisation, these enterprises became substantial contributors to total income tax collections. When the demands from state enterprises for capital and subsidies are reduced, government is able to spend more on public services such as hospitals and schools.

### *Utilise New Technology*

Political considerations tend to constrain the ability of state-owned enterprises to function efficiently and respond to new developments. Once in the private sector, they are free to make purely commercial decisions regarding the implementation of new technologies and the utilisation of outside expertise.

### *Motivate the Workforce*

Most state-owned enterprises are over-staffed and have poorly motivated employees. Attendance records compare poorly with those in the private sector and the incidence of sickness is higher, which are signs of low morale. In the private sector, the corporate culture and more rapid recognition of effort and ability in privatised enterprises is found to boost morale and delivery of customer service.

## Nationalisation Case Studies

A detailed analysis follows of selected nationalisation attempts from across the globe over different time periods.

Attempts at nationalisation reveal that whenever government involves itself with business, it unleashes a conflicting mix of social and efficiency objectives. To justify nationalisation, governments invariably make a raft of promises to voters but when faced with difficult but necessary decisions, often driven by changes internationally, they default on those promises. As the case studies show, these promises do not come without their consequences and inflict damage on the domestic economy. The decision to nationalise is all the more perplexing because, in all cases, the government receives significant revenues from the private companies without carrying any of the associated risks involved in operating a business.

### *Zambia: Case Study*

According to the ANCYL *Discussion Document* (2010:21), "The last potential challenge to nationalisation of Mines in South Africa will be the lame reference to the failed State-Owned Copper Mines in countries such as Zambia".[8] But Zambia provides important lessons about government involvement in industry.

In 1964, when Zambia gained its independence, its newly appointed leaders wanted to create a better life for all of its citizens. Like the current ANCYL, the Zambian government thought that by controlling the copper companies they would be able to achieve their developmental goals with the revenues derived from mining operations. According to Libby and Woakes, "[Zambia's] Leaders appeared to see the government's ownership of the copper companies as being a relatively cost free way to develop the country".[9]

However, when the world price of copper dropped unexpectedly in the mid-1970s (see Copper Prices graph below), it put the fiscus under immense pressure and Zambia was plunged into debt as the government attempted to sustain the now unprofitable mining operations. The government was forced to make some painful decisions, the cost of which ultimately came at the expense of development in other sectors of the economy.

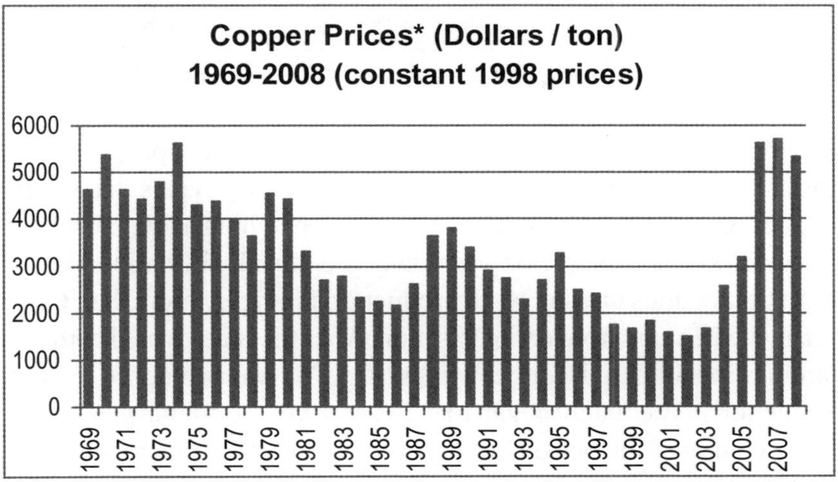


*Unit value is estimated from the "Annual Average US Producer Copper Price" as reported in the Minerals Prices 98 and the 2006 Minerals Yearbook

Source: US Geological Survey, 2009 – available at: http://minerals.usgs.gov/ds/2005/140/copper.pdf

The reduction in the revenues derived from Zambia's primary export, which accounted for two-thirds of the country's income, can be seen in the declining level of income per capita. In 1964, Zambia had a GDP per capita of $554 in constant 2000 prices, making it one of the richest sub-Saharan African countries at the time. More than four decades later, it is ranked amongst the poorest, with a real income per capita of $400, roughly the same amount as the late-1980s (see GDP per Capita graph below).

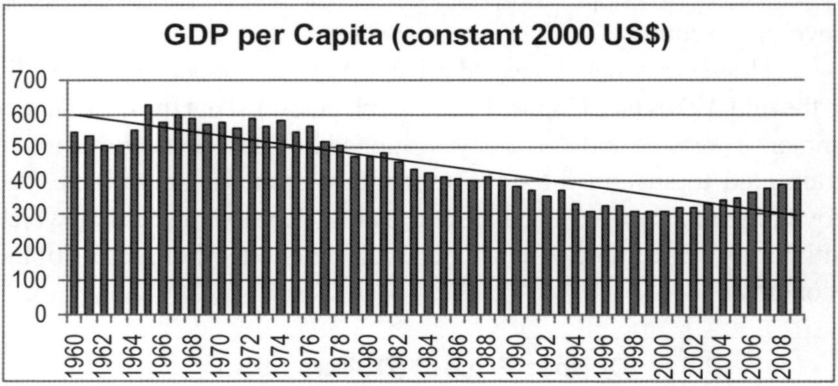


Source: World Bank, World Development Indicators, 2010

In 1969, when the mines were nationalised, Zambia's copper production was at its peak, at 720,000 tons. The graph below reveals that copper production declined dramatically thereafter, reaching a low of 241,000 tons in 2000 when the sector was finally privatised. The nationalisation was a tremendous disaster, with production falling by more than 63 per cent in the 27 years from nationalisation. After the state-owned company Zambia Consolidated Copper Mines (ZCCM) was privatised in 2000, production immediately began to increase. Average annual growth was 11 per cent over the period 2000-2008. In 2008, Zambia regained the level of copper output it had achieved in 1980 and according to Zambia's mining minister, Maxwell Mwhale, "In 2010, we are projecting that [production] should get to about 750,000 metric tonnes. That was a figure last achieved in 1973".[10]

Its shrinking proportion of world copper production depicts an even clearer indication of the decline in Zambia's copper output after nationalisation. As a percentage of total world production, Zambia's copper output fell from 12.1 per cent in 1969 to 1.8 per cent in 2000. Thereafter, when the sector was privatised in 2000, its share of world production began to increase steadily up to its present contribution of approximately 3 per cent.

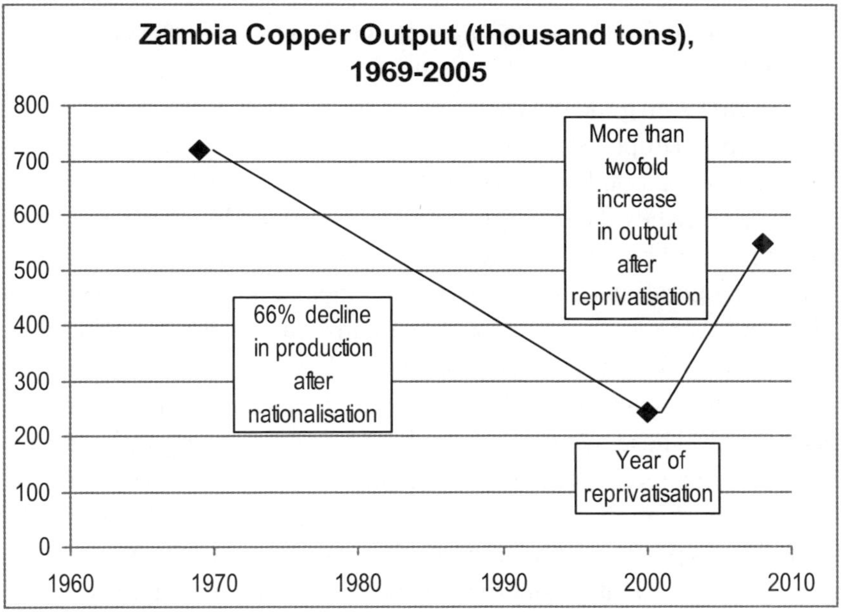


Source: US Geological Survey, 2010

The Zambian case demonstrates the conflicting mix of social- and efficiency- objectives that arises when government gets involved in industry. The Zambian government's 1969 decision to nationalise the mining companies by taking a 51 per cent ownership, created an unbearable financial obligation that did not exist before. For as long as the world price of copper remained high and the copper industry made profits, the government did not concern itself with the financial burdens of supporting the mining industry. However, when the world price of copper began to decline in the mid-1970s and reached the point where the industry was no longer self-financing and actually had to resort to borrowing merely to operate, the financial burden fell squarely at the feet of the Zambian government. As the majority shareholder, the Zambian government was forced to guarantee loans and inject large sums of money into the companies to keep them afloat.

In the face of the rising costs of production, private companies would have reacted faster and more efficiently. However, the government had made promises to the electorate and had other obligations that did not coincide with good business practices. If it had not assumed majority ownership and imposed restrictions on the mining companies , they would have no doubt responded very differently to the rising costs by, for example, curtailing activities at the marginal mines or even mothballing them until it became profitable to operate them again. Instead, the government continued operations at these marginal mines even though, according to Libby and Woakes, "… mines such as Luanshya… had been losing about 500 [Kwacha] for every ton of copper produced… (and) the Kansanshi mine was losing about 840 [Kwacha] for every ton of finished copper produced".[11] These two mines were kept in operation largely because of the government's commitment to guarantee employment to the miners.

As production costs rose, the Zambian government found itself in the invidious position of having to bail out a non-profitable sector again and again. The country sank further and further into debt merely to keep the mining industry in operation and guarantee employment to the miners. Of course, the mounting debt came at the expense of investment in other developmental areas.

If, instead of nationalising the mines, the government had raised the revenue it needed via the tax system, it would have had the finances to invest in other areas of society. By nationalising the mines, it was forced to divert government finances to the mining industry and had no funding for other purposes.

### *Botswana: Case Study*

In the ANCYL *Discussion Document*, under the section "Nationalisation to increase the State's fiscal capacity and better the working conditions", Botswana is presented as a case "on why nationalisation of strategic minerals can benefit the South African State".[12] At the outset it must be noted that Botswana's mining operations comprise a joint initiative between the private sector and Botswana's government. A partnership recognised by the ANCYL when it says, "In Botswana, the State is in a 50% each partnership with De Beers in a mining joint venture called Debswana Diamond Company Ltd".

More importantly, according to Modise, the Deputy Permanent Secretary of the President in Botswana, "All major mining ventures in Botswana have always been run as private companies in which Government has significant shareholding... In the case of Botswana, Government has had an arm's length approach in the day-to-day operations of the mining companies".[13]

Indeed, when Botswana first discovered diamonds in 1967, one year into independence, it faced the task of attracting investors and increasing the welfare of its citizens. Potential investors like De Beers faced considerable risk by counting on Botswana's newly formed government to adhere to consistent policies over time.

In order to attract these potential investors, the government committed itself to providing a predictable environment in which the mining companies could operate. For example, it introduced a stable tax regime and made a commitment to maintain a stable regulatory environment and, most importantly, not to nationalise operations. The result was a profit-sharing arrangement that gave both parties a stake in the continuing success of the mining operations. This revenue sharing agreement has benefited both parties and, because of this, encouraged further investment.[14]

Botswana's diamond mining success is thus based on a sound institutional framework and participation by the private sector. It, therefore, definitely cannot be seen as a case for nationalisation. Yet, despite this, the ANCYL document states, "... the Botswana model of ownership...

is an important lesson, which should be considered in South Africa's transfer of minerals wealth to the ownership of the people as a whole".

We have to agree with that statement, except that it would not be a case of nationalising the mining industry, but rather one of enriching the people by allowing the private sector more freedom to influence government involvement and maximise profits in the industry.

Botswana's current model, however, is not sustainable. Diamond mining accounts for over 38 per cent of GDP and over one-third of the government's revenues.[15]

With the government receiving revenue from mining activities, a paradox has emerged where there is a high level of government expenditure but a low level of taxation. This leads the majority of people in Botswana to think that they are getting something for nothing. They do not realise that the services currently provided by the government are being funded by revenue from diamonds as opposed to taxes.

Despite Botswana's relatively high level of national income, which ranks it amongst upper-middle income countries, the country still suffers from many characteristically low-income country problems such as high levels of poverty and unemployment. According to the United Nations Development Programme, 47 per cent of the population lives below the national poverty line[16] and although the official rate of unemployment was 7.5 per cent in 2007, the unofficial estimate is closer to 40 per cent.[17] These high levels of poverty and unemployment are largely the result of the reliance on government revenue originating from one dominant sector, namely, diamond mining.

In an economy, private sector investment is the real driver of growth and employment. A government's high levels of spending crowd out private sector investment and inhibit future economic development by perpetuating resource dependency. Moreover, now that diamond revenues have stabilised (see Mineral Revenue graph below) and are expected to decline within the next few decades, the current size and scope of Botswana's public sector is not only unsustainable, but also undesirable if it is to switch to a more balanced and modern economy. Considering the low level of private activity in the economy and the resultant relatively low tax base,

Botswana's welfare hangs in a precarious balance. The government needs to diversify the economy by creating the conditions necessary for the private sector to thrive and to reduce its reliance on an exhaustible resource.

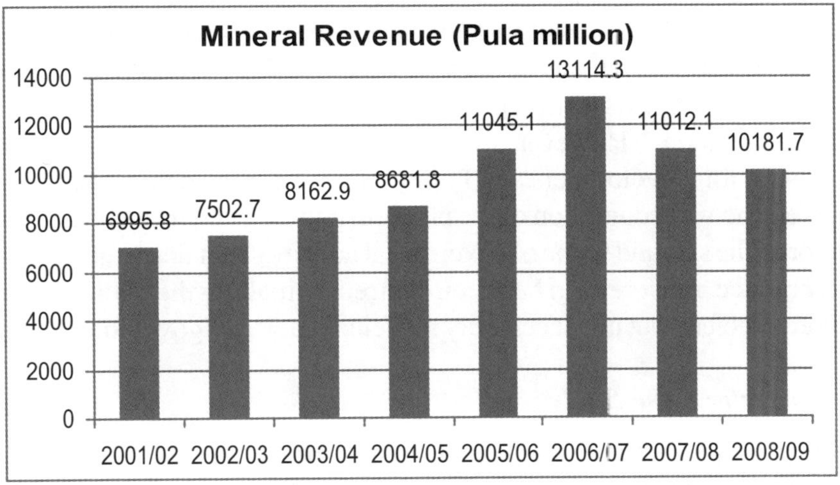


Source: Ministry of Finance and Development Planning, September 2010

Contrary to the ANCYL's view, the Botswana case demonstrates that less government involvement is required. In the long run, the only way to resolve the high degree of dependence on government revenue is to reduce the size and scope of government. Declining diamond revenues mean that Botswana's government is soon going have to make some painful decisions. Considering its small tax base, services will have to be significantly curtailed or, like the case of Zambia, it risks sinking itself under a mountain of debt.

Concern about Botswana's economy is not a new issue. Several reports in recent years have mentioned the dubious sustainability of the size and structure of the public sector in Botswana. The 1997 World Bank *World Development Report* and a 2000 report by the Royal Norwegian Ministry of Foreign Affairs (with the Botswana Institute for Development and Policy Analysis – BIDPA) both examined the problem caused by the size of the government. The finding of both reports was that the government agencies were fulfilling roles that could easily, and in many cases, more effectively be performed by the private sector.[18]

The government is well aware of these concerns. Botswana's "National Development Plan 8" declared "The current size and structure of the public sector are not sustainable and measures will be put in place to 'right-size' and rationalise the public sector". The government has also included within its national strategy the need for privatisation and decentralisation.[19] However, a study conducted in 2004 by the Botswana Institute for Development and Policy Analysis showed that despite the government's recognition of the problem and the need for public sector reform, the size and scope of government activities remained unchanged. In practice, most reform has been centred on making the public sector more efficient, but not necessarily reducing the size of government.[20]

### *Venezuela: Case Study*

Since oil production first began on a commercial scale in 1917 in Venezuela, it has been the main driver of economic activity.[21] Currently it is responsible for about 30 per cent of Venezuela's GDP, 50 per cent of the government's revenue and 80 per cent of its export earnings.[22] Over-reliance on this one commodity, though, has created a number of perverse incentives and unintended consequences that come largely at the expense of the welfare of Venezuela's citizens.

Venezuela has a classic case of "Dutch Disease", a phrase coined after the discovery of natural gas in the Netherlands in the late 1950s. When the economy increasingly relied on natural gas revenues to fund development, it resulted in a decline in the manufacturing sector and halted development in other sectors of the economy. Venezuela's fortunes are thus largely hinged on a high oil price and in order to stabilise prices, Venezuela was instrumental in the establishment of the Organisation of the Petroleum Exporting Countries (OPEC). The main goal of OPEC is to stabilise the price of oil by restricting the available supply.

*Nationalisation*

In 1971, under the presidency of Rafael Caldera, a law was passed which stated that all assets, plant and equipment belonging to concessionaires would revert to the nation without compensation upon the expiration of the concession.[23] This was the first decisive step down the road of nationalisation. The "1973 Oil Crisis", which led to a dramatic surge in oil prices, emboldened Venezuela's subsequent president Carlos Perez to embark on a nationalisation programme driven by the windfall profits received from oil revenues (see Crude Oil Refiner Acquisition Costs graph below). Following the typical cycle of nationalisations – to nationalise when the price of a commodity is high – by 1976, the oil industry was completely nationalised. All foreign-owned oil companies had been replaced by Venezuelan companies and the state-run oil company, Petroleos de Venezuela SA (PDVSA), had been established.

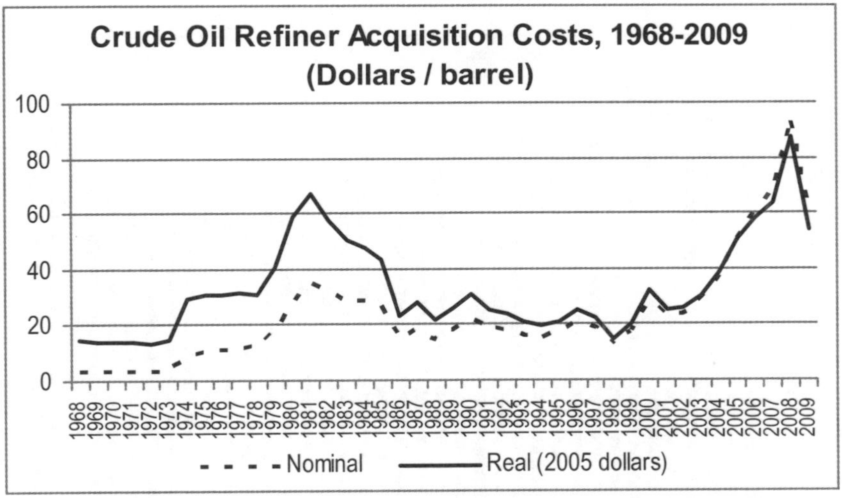


Source: US Energy Information Administration, International Energy Statistics

Venezuela also followed a policy of import substitution industrialisation (ISI) and was granting generous subsidies to "special" economic sectors. The ISI strategy, effectively funded by oil revenues, shielded local manufacturers from foreign competition in an attempt to diversify the economy away from the over-reliance on oil. However, these protectionist measures failed to improve their efficiency and these local industries remain under-developed to this day.

These inefficient local industries, hiding behind protectionist barriers, have consumed resources that could have been used more efficiently elsewhere in the economy by the private sector if it had been allowed to do so. Not surprisingly, GDP per capita in Venezuela has languished at relatively low levels since the early 1970s and remains relatively unchanged (see GDP per Capita graph below).

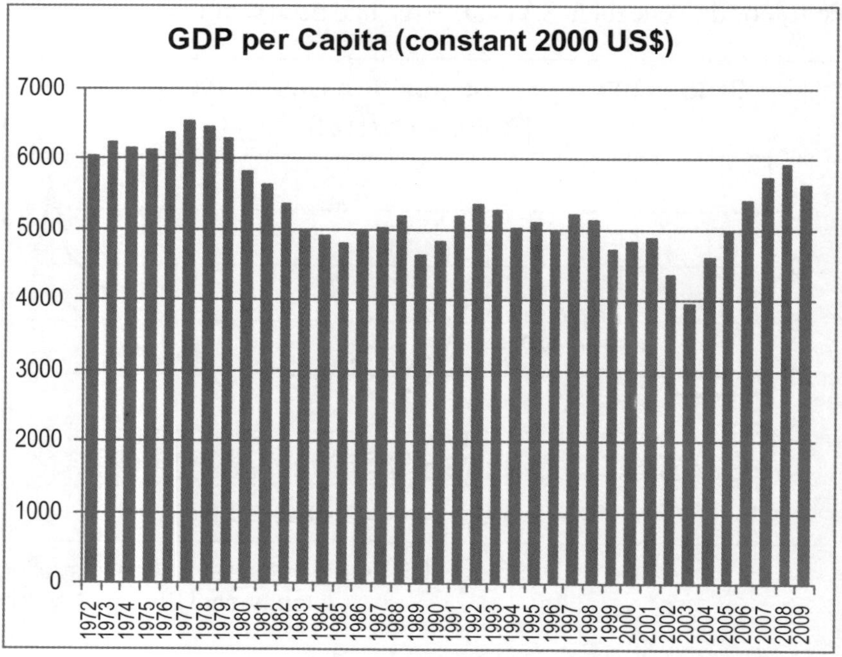


Source: World Bank, World Development Indicators, 2010

Venezuela's citizens have suffered under these failed economic polices. The country has witnessed some of the highest levels of inflation over protracted periods. Throughout the 1960s and 1970s inflation was kept low and stable (see Inflation, Consumer Prices graph below), but, as the price of oil declined from a high in the early 1980s, revenues dried up and the government resorted to printing money in order to maintain its welfare spending. This led to a significant rise in inflation. Compared to the period 1961 to 1980 when inflation averaged 4.8 per cent, from 1981 to 1990, the average was 24.9 per cent. Inflation then increased dramatically, peaking at roughly 100 per cent in 1996. Over the period 1990 to 2009, inflation averaged at 34.3 per cent.

When there is high inflation, people cannot make rational economic decisions. They are more concerned with seeking out ways to maintain their wealth. Invariably, people make poor investment decisions when they rush to invest in anything available in an effort to benefit as much as possible before the value of their money is eroded. In a high inflation environment it also becomes impossible to save because inflation benefits borrowers at the expense of savers.

Savings are imperative for any economy. Without savings there is no investment. Without investment, the productivity of the economy and individuals cannot increase. Without increased productivity, wages cannot rise. This all leads to a crash in savings and completes the vicious downward spiral.

Import-substituting policies and high levels of inflation have imposed substantial costs on Venezuela's consumers and have greatly reduced the well-being of its citizens. But these results are entirely predictable and are the result of an undemocratic society that significantly curtails economic and political freedoms.

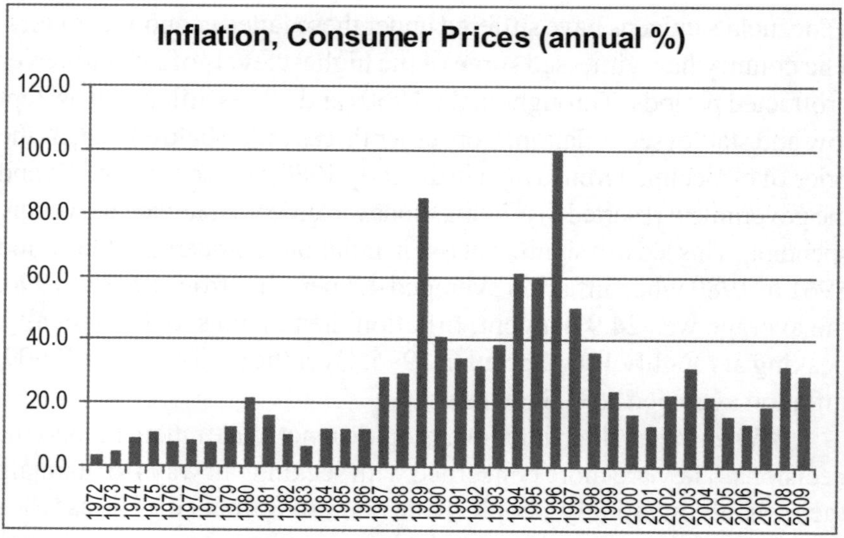


Source: World Bank, World Development Indicators, 2010

In the 1990s, Venezuela did open its doors to private investment and allow foreign companies to manage specific oil fields. But in 1999, dictator Hugo Chávez took office and pushed through a new constitution that gave his government the right to nationalise any company it deemed to be "in the national interest".[24] Within a year, trading volumes on Venezuela's Stock Exchange tumbled by approximately 30 per cent from their levels three years prior to the announcements.[25]

In 2001, state control over the economy increased when the government imposed a new tax on oil and required all new foreign petroleum ventures to be governmentally controlled.[26,27] In December 2002, the Venezuelan economy experienced a dramatic downturn following a failed military coup to overthrow Chávez. The state-run oil company PDVSA went on a two-month long strike, which ultimately caused the economy to contract by 8.9 per cent in 2002 and 7.8 per cent in 2003.[28] According to some estimates, as many as 19,000 people were dismissed from PDVSA in the aftermath of the strike and replaced with workers loyal to the Chávez government.[29] Not surprisingly, oil production declined significantly over this period and still has not recovered to the levels produced prior to 2002 (see Total Oil Production graph below).

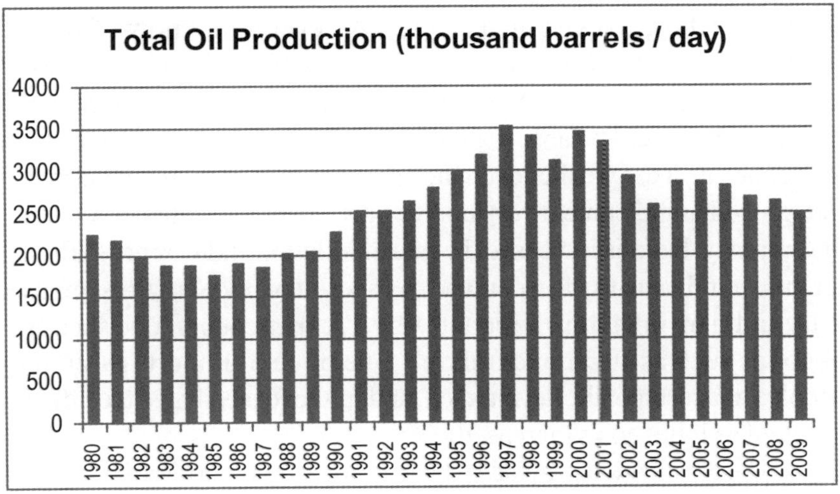


Source: US Energy Information Administration, International Energy Statistics

*The Consequences of Nationalisation*

Francisco Rodriguez, former chief economist of the Venezuelan National Assembly, wrote in a 2008 *Foreign Affairs* article that income inequality increased during Chávez's tenure, and further, that Chávez's social programmes have not had a major impact on infant mortality or literacy rates among Venezuelans.[30] Under Chávez, the state-run oil company PDVSA's mandate has drastically expanded to include the government's social priorities. For example, it is legislated that PDVSA must spend at least 10 per cent of its annual investment budget on social programmes.[31]

As mentioned previously, inflation is rampant. The Venezuelan bolivar is in free fall because Chávez has resorted to printing money to fund his dictatorship. Writing for the *Wall Street Journal* (WSJ) Mary Anastasia O'Grady says, "It's no secret that his popularity, despite the deterioration in Venezuelan living standards, comes from printing and spreading bolivars around low-income barrios as well as among nouveau-riche business elites and the military".[32]

At the beginning of this year, Chávez announced that the bolivar would be devalued from 2.15 to 4.30 to the dollar for non-essential goods (such as radios, television sets, etc). As everyone knows from the experience of Zimbabwe, you cannot interfere with the market without there being consequences. Despite Chávez's assertions that the Venezuelan government would be able to provide all the dollars needed to operate the economy at the weaker exchange rate, the lack of oil revenue caused foreign exchange sources to dry up. He subsequently resorted to devaluing the currency, but this increased the rate of inflation and was not sufficient for the central bank to meet demand. As a result of price controls imposed to try and stem inflation, the country is "... experiencing food shortages of goods such as sugar and milk".[33] The price of imports essentially doubled as a result of the devaluation, and further exacerbated the inflation problem as input costs increased.

The devaluation provided Chávez with a temporary breathing space because he effectively earns twice as many bolivars for every dollar he receives from oil revenues. But, according to reports in the WSJ, "With too many *bolivars* chasing too few goods, Mr. Chávez is now blaming 'speculators' [for the country's inflation]. Recently he arrested 47 butchers for evading his price controls".[34] In an all too familiar scenario, reminiscent of Zimbabwe's inflationary woes, the WSJ also notes, "The Congress [Chávez] controls, has... proposed legislation to criminalize trading in the parallel market for dollars. Yet beyond terrorizing the nation, the crackdown is unlikely to improve things because the market needs dollars to function".[35]

In the *Economic Freedom of the World 2010 Annual Report* (EFW), it is said that as economic freedom declines, homicide rates increase and notes that this negative relationship is nowhere more apparent than in Venezuela. Stringham and Levendis state, "Over the last two decades, Venezuela has seen an erratic but downward trend in economic freedom and an increase in homicides... The years 2001 to 2003 witnessed a massive drop of 38% in economic freedom (from 5.49 to 3.99) and a simultaneous 38% increase in murder rates (from 32 to 44 per 100,000 residents)".[36] According to the NGO, The Venezuelan Observatory of Violence, homicides have quadrupled during Chávez's 11 years in power, with two people murdered every hour.[37]

### *Bolivia: Case Study*

In spite of having the region's second largest natural gas reserves after Venezuela, Bolivia is among Latin America's poorest nations with a GDP per capita of $1,192 in 2009 (see GDP per Capita graph below), compared to the regional average of $4,780 (measured in constant 2000 prices). According to the CIA, approximately 60 per cent of the population lived below the poverty line in 2006.[38] Moreover, life expectancy at birth has remained low and static for several decades and the average individual can only expect to live to age 65. As will be shown below, the Bolivian hydrocarbons industry has been plagued with uncertainty as the various political regimes have rotated between varying degrees of respect and lack of respect for private property rights. This uncertainty has restricted the amount of investment entering the Bolivian economy and all sectors have suffered as a result. The hydrocarbons industry, which requires massive investment, has never reached its full potential due to this uncertainty and the constant threat of nationalisation.

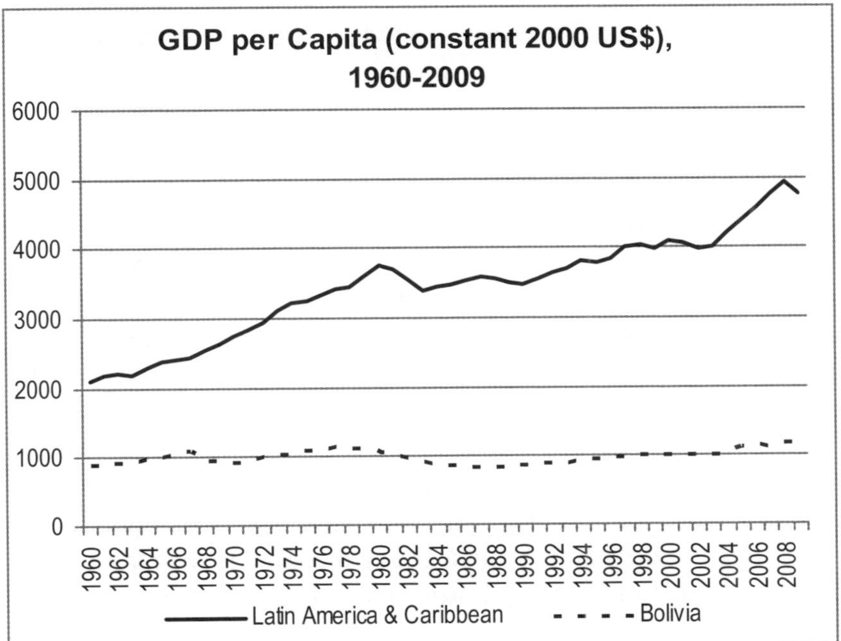


Source: World Bank, World Development Indicators, 2010

*History of Hydrocarbons in Bolivia*

Bolivia's first oil well was built by the Standard Oil Company in 1922 and in 1924 its first oil field began production. However, in 1936, after several years of profitable operations, Colonel David Toro established the state-owned petroleum company, Bolivian Fiscal Oil Fields (YPFB, its Spanish abbreviation). The following year, Toro's government confiscated all of Standard Oil Company's holdings – effectively nationalising Bolivia's petroleum industry.

According to Chang *et al*, "In 1952, the Nationalist Revolutionary Movement (MNR) overthrew a military regime and conducted a revolutionary program that granted universal suffrage, implemented agrarian and educational reform, and nationalized the country's mines. Contrary to government expectations, however, agricultural output dropped, tin production halved, the country experienced inflation rates of 900%, and hydrocarbon production was well below potential".[39]

Bolivia's economic and social woes continued as the country followed a nationalist agenda, which ultimately prompted a regime change. In 1956, Hernán Siles Zuazo was elected president. He amended existing legislation to again allow foreign companies to own property. This encouraged new investment from foreign companies and in 1961 the foreign-owned Gulf Oil Company discovered vast natural gas and petroleum reserves. According to Chang *et al*, "... the large investments in exploration, extraction, and distribution of hydrocarbons were paying off, as production improved sharply and profits increased several fold".[40]

In 1969, Alfredo Obando seized government control through a military coup and shortly thereafter nationalised Gulf Oil. Although private operators were allowed a limited role in the industry, relatively little extraction and exploration took place due again to uncertainty in the economy. However, in yet another reversal, Chang *et al* note, "[In 1972] ... the government passed the General Hydrocarbon Law to promote foreign investment, even if government retained property rights".[41] As a result, the private sector again negotiated contracts with the state-run company YPFB and began exporting natural gas to Argentina.

In the late 1970s and early to mid-1980s, Bolivia recorded several years of negative economic growth rates as a result of political disruptions that witnessed the presidency change no less than nine times over a short period of time. Political uncertainty did not come without its consequences and in 1985 inflation reached 11,750 per cent. That same year, Bolivia elected a new president, Victor Estenssoro, who introduced "The New Economic Policy", which "froze wages, raised the price of fuel, devalued the Bolivian peso, eliminated price supports and laid off approximately 80 per cent of the mining work force".[42] Inflation dropped to 276 per cent the following year and then to 15 per cent in 1987. However, as the Natural Gas Production graph below depicts, despite the reforms introduced by President Estenssoro, natural gas production remained low and stagnant throughout the early 1980s. According to Chang *et al* the reason for this "... was due to the weak incentives that nationalized ownership implied".[43]

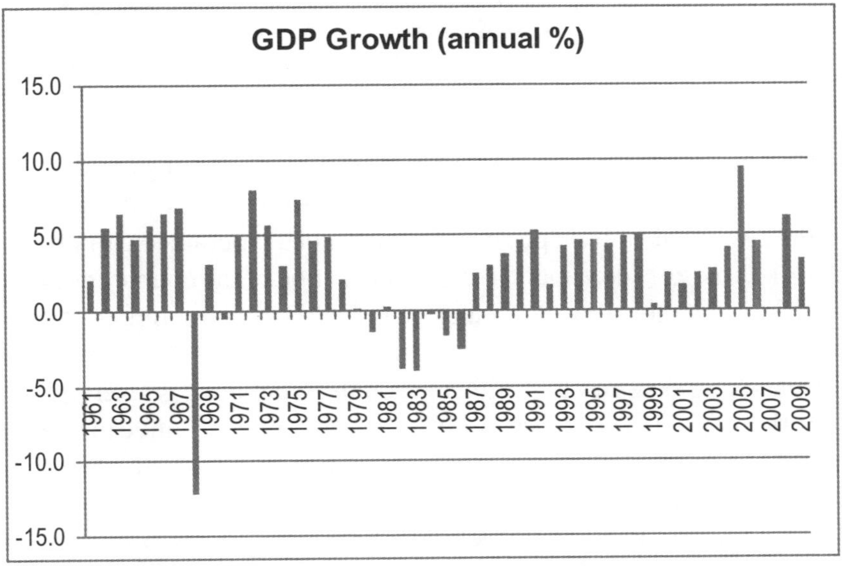


Source: World Bank, World Development Indicators, 2010

In 1993, Gonzalo Sanchez de Lozada won the presidency by promising to privatise the sluggish and inefficient state-run hydrocarbons industry. Shortly thereafter the hydrocarbons sector began attracting increasing amounts of foreign investment and production began to steadily increase.

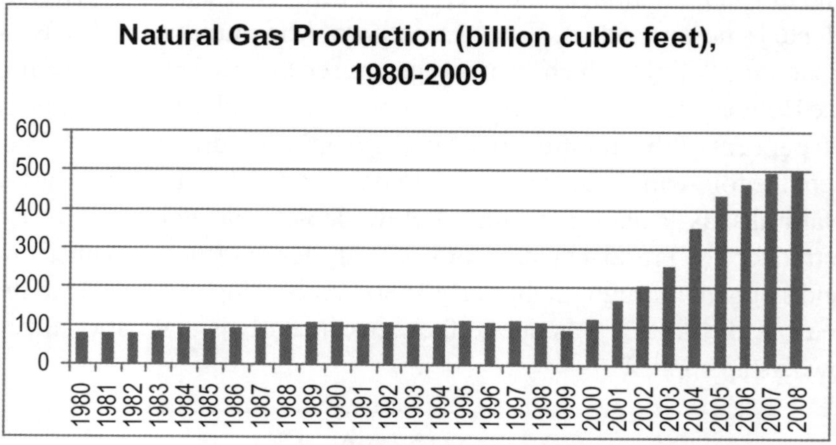


Source: US Energy Information Administration, International Energy Statistics

Gas prices began a slow recovery in 1995 after stagnating at relatively low levels for several years. However, in 1998, civil unrest increased due to the news that Bolivia planned to construct a pipeline to carry gas to Brazil. Protestors demanded the nationalisation of the country's natural gas resources. According to Chang *et al*, "The Bolivian component alone had cost $550 million… [and] was also a testament to the sizeable sunk investments necessary to exploit the country's natural gas reserves". As the price of gas began to rise in 1999, the economic incentive to explore increased and proved reserves grew from approximately 4 tcf (trillion cubic feet) in 2000 to 18 tcf in 2001.

Tensions peaked in October 2003 when riots broke out in opposition to the potential construction of a gas pipeline to Chile. President Sanchez de Lozada was forced to resign and Vice President Carlos Mesa took over. In 2004, amidst calls for nationalisation of the hydrocarbons sector, President Mesa held a referendum on property rights. Despite this referendum, violent protests broke out and Mesa was also forced to resign.

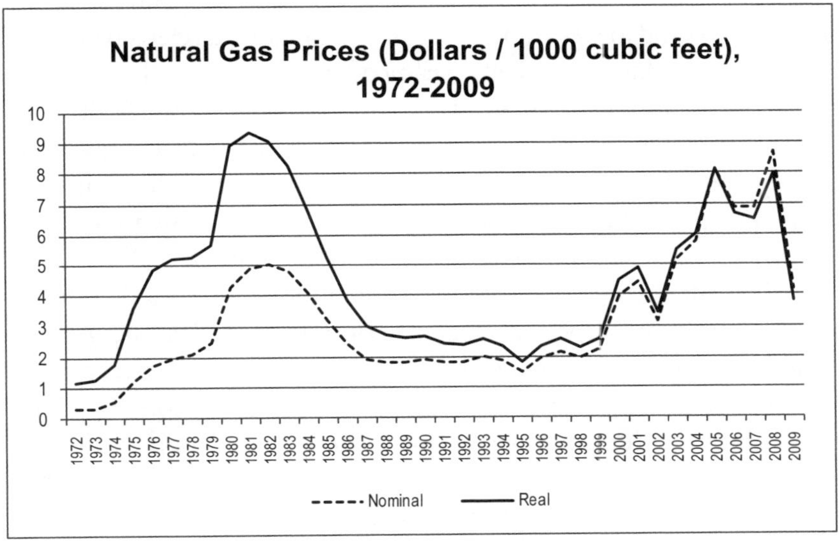


Source: US Energy Information Administration, International Energy Statistics

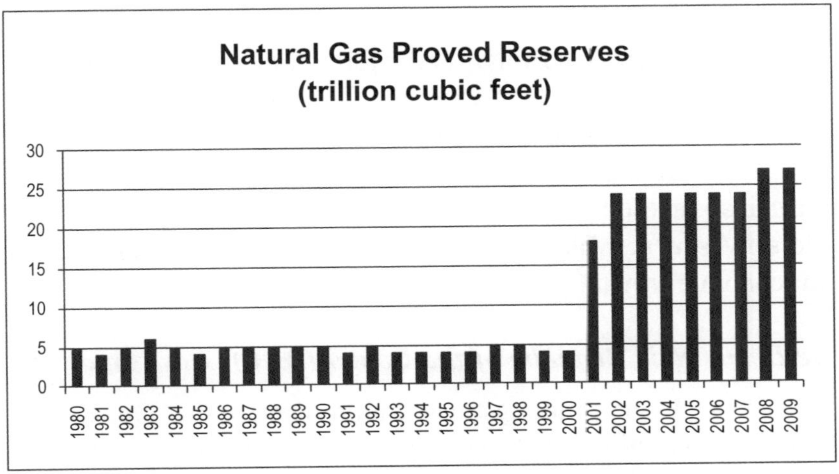


Source: US Energy Information Administration, International Energy Statistics

Because the Bolivian government collected revenues through fixed royalty payments, its share of revenue remained static despite increased production and price. Lower than expected revenues yet again contributed to civil unrest and in December 2005, Evo Morales was elected president after promising during his election campaign to nationalise the gas and oil industries. According to Chang *et al*, "Amidst rising gas prices, declining fiscal contribution of the gas companies, and increasing inequality, he had gained popularity by campaigning on a platform of nationalization... FDI and investment in the energy sector had been trending down since 1999, and in the year of Morales' election they both plummeted".[44]

Despite the fact that foreign companies had invested almost $4 billion in the hydrocarbons sector since Bolivia opened its energy sector in the 1990s, Morales nationalised Bolivia's gas and oil industry in May 2006. He gave foreign investors a six-month deadline to comply with the government's demands or leave.[45] More specifically, Morales' nationalisation decree stated that all foreign-owned companies must hand over majority control of their companies to the state-owned company YPFB and were given 180 days to renegotiate their energy contracts with the Bolivian state.[46] Also, during this period, the largest foreign-owned companies were slapped with a 32 per cent hike in royalties and taxes.

Experts warn that Bolivia needs foreign-owned companies, such as Brazil's Petrobras, which accounts for roughly 20 per cent of the country's GDP and 24 per cent of its tax revenue.[47] Morales' actions are extremely short-sighted because, although Bolivia may see some short-term gains as a result of increased tax revenues, in the long-run there will be less investment, which is the ultimate driver of increased productivity and economic growth.

### *The Democratic Republic of the Congo (DRC): Case Study*

The private Belgian mining trust, Union Miniere du Haut Katanga (UMHK), was nationalised by then President Mobutu Sese Seko on 31 December 1966[48] , as part of a programme to bring the "political and economic centre of gravity back home" and "re-establish the autonomy of the Congo as a 'popular' nationalist project"[49] forming the new mining giant Gécamines (Générale de Carrières et des Mines).

Most of the former management and technical employees were retained to staff the "Société Générale des Minerais". This separate entity "was to take care of all the servicing required for the operation of the nationalised company, including employment of personnel, and industrial and commercial management of the company".[50] For this period, the company, although officially nationalised, effectively operated like a private entity. Nonetheless, over time the employees who had been retained, were steadily replaced by political cronies up to the beginning of the decline of the company in 1989.[51]

The following table illustrates the result of Congolese mine nationalisation by comparing the production figures of Gécamines for the years 1989 to 2003.

**DRC Table 1**: Gécamines Mineral Production (Tons) 1989-2003

| Year | Copper | Zinc | Cobalt |
|---|---|---|---|
| 1989 | 440,848 | 54,043 | - |
| 1990 | 376,000 | - | - |
| 1991 | 240,000 | 30,000 | 9,800 |
| 1994 | 32,412 | 2515 | 3,631 |
| 2001 | 27,507 | - | 3,463 |
| 2002 | 21,186 | 828 | 1,780 |
| 2003 | 16,172 | - | 1,200 |

Source: http://en.wikipedia.org/wiki/G%C3%A9camines

Between 1989 and 2003 copper production declined by 96 per cent, zinc by 99 per cent, and between 1991 and 2003 the production of cobalt declined by 88 per cent.

The dramatic decline in Gécamines Copper, Zinc and Cobalt output following nationalisation can be seen in the graphs below:

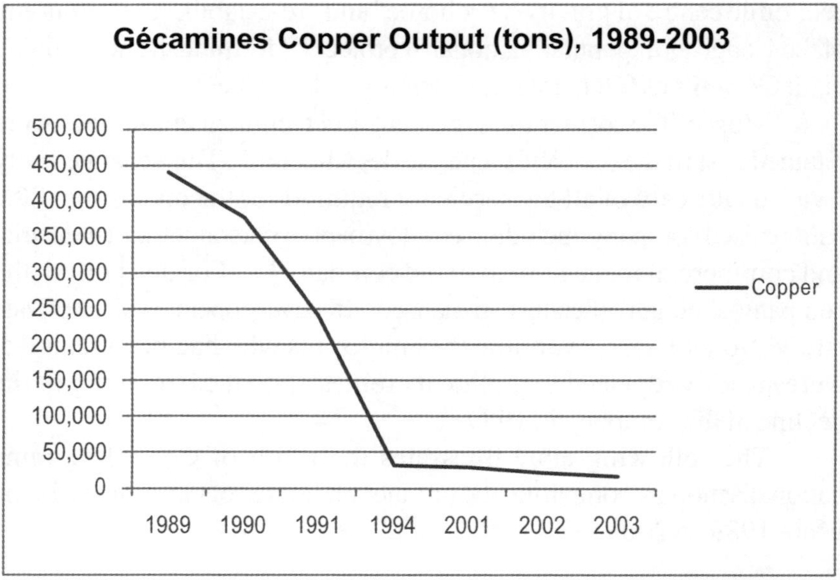


Source: DRC Table 1

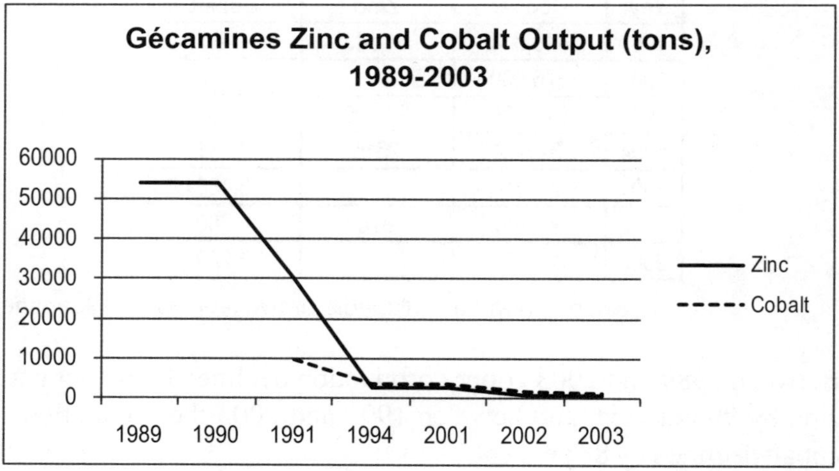


Source: DRC Table 1

The implication of these figures is staggering. What they are telling us is that as soon as the Congolese mines were fully and properly nationalised, production fell dramatically, which brought about associated declines in national income, GDP, government tax revenue, human development and broad national stability. One analyst describes the Zaire[52] mine nationalisation as follows: "Most foreign investors fled and those who stayed behind turned their attention to making quick profits, which they then repatriated overseas. Prior to 1974 the Zairian economy grew at 7 per cent per year. Following nationalisation, the country started on a downward spiral that continues to this day. In 2006, the Congo was the third poorest country in sub-Saharan Africa. Congolese incomes were 23 times lower than those of Seychellois – Africa's richest people". The effects of nationalisation extended beyond the immediate economic crisis. "The belief that something could be had for nothing ... had been endorsed at the very highest level of society. Mobutu Sese Seko and his ministers had plundered mercilessly, and no one had ever been punished. Zaire became a kleptocracy and Mobutu Sese Seko was the kleptocrat-in-chief. The extent of his loot became legendary."[53]

A Reuters report in *Mining Weekly* on 22 November 2010, "DRC sacks Gécamines top management – officials", reveals that the problems at Gécamines continue:

> "At its peak in the late 1980s, Gécamines produced more than 470,000 tons of copper and more than 13,000 tons of cobalt. But the decline in the company's fortunes mirrored those of the country, which saw rampant corruption under the late president Mobutu Sese Seko, followed by two wars in the 1990s. A peace deal in 2003, elections in 2006 and high metals prices have seen mining firms return to Katanga but Gécamines' share of business remains low following a world collapse of prices after the 2008-2009 financial and economic crisis. Leaving aside production from joint ventures copper and cobalt output were 13,367t and 495t, respectively, in 2009, according to the firm's 2009 annual report, which cited delays in revamping equipment. Outgoing Gécamines director Mukasa told Reuters last week that

Gécamines has accumulated $1,5-billion in debt following years of mismanagement under Mobutu. Of that, he said, the company owed more than $300-million in unpaid salaries and worker dues, $300 million for national power company SNEL and more than $300-million on unpaid taxes."[54]

Meanwhile, the Congo has permitted some private mining ventures, which are operating successfully, such as Metorex Ltd's Ruashi mine.

"Metorex Ltd, which mines copper in Africa, said output at its Ruashi mine rose to its highest level last month, with copper production 21 per cent higher and cobalt gaining 33 per cent. 'The Ruashi mine continues to improve throughput and production levels,' Chief Executive Terence Goodlace said in a statement to the Stock Exchange News Service in Johannesburg. The Ruashi mine is in the Democratic Republic of Congo. Metorex said on August 21 it will spend as much as US$400 million over the next five years to boost output of the metal more than five-fold. Copper output may climb to 140,000t by 2012 from 25,350t in the year ended June 30 and cobalt production may increase to 8,000t from 565t. Output of copper in May was 1,847t, .... Cobalt production was 214t."[55]

### *Chile: Case Study*

Chile undertook a 16-year process of nationalisation between 1955 and 1971[56], merging all previous mining companies into a single state conglomerate called Codelco. One of the two major mining companies in Chile at the time, Anaconda Copper Mines, saw a 66 per cent decline in copper output following nationalisation.[57]

In 1983, Chile reformed its stagnating mining sector by introducing a new code which restored property rights and private participation. While remaining a state-owned enterprise, Codelco began to launch partnerships with private firms. More recently, private mining companies started opening mines elsewhere in the country, and, today, continue to expand and increase production. Codelco's share of Chilean mining output has fallen dramatically. In 1990, its share of Chilean copper production was 75 per cent and in 2009, only 32 per cent.

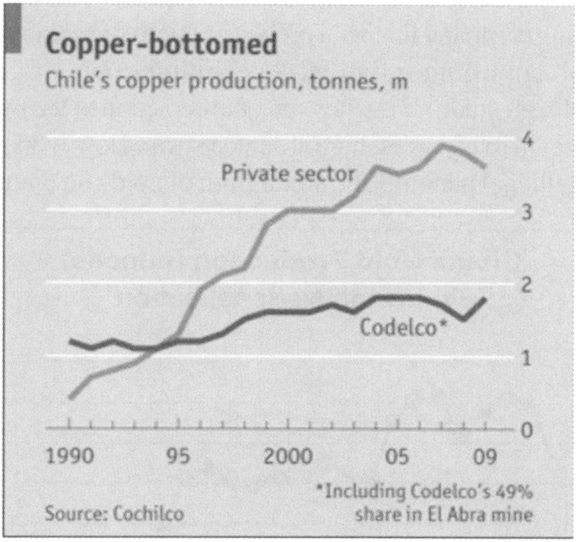


Source: The Economist, 21 October 2010, "Reviving Codelco" [58]

Codelco's output has remained relatively stagnant at 1.6m tons for the last 10 years. The Chilean President, Sebastián Piñera, has often criticised Codelco for its "inefficiency, griping over its stagnant output and climbing costs". He has also expressed his desire to privatise Codelco and has made significant reforms that mimic privatisation. According to *The Economist*, "Its board now has more independence from the government; the directors recruited Diego Hernández, a former manager at BHP Billiton, the world's biggest mining company, as the new chief executive".[59]

### *Ghana: Case Study*

Ghana nationalised its mining sector in the early 1960s with the objective of "maximising government revenue ... and employment generation". [60] Instead, the industry experienced a dramatic decline following nationalisation, with gold production falling from 915,317 ounces in 1960 to 282,299 ounces by 1984.[61] The reasons given by the World Bank for the decline were a "lack of foreign exchange to maintain and rehabilitate the mines; lack of capital investment for mining skills; infrastructure deterioration, particularly shortages of rail capacity for manganese and bauxite; mining company financial problems due to the greatly over-valued currency and spiralling inflation; a declining grade of gold ore; the exhaustion of high grade manganese ore; the depletion of the more lucrative diamond mines in many areas; high absenteeism and low worker discipline; and pilfering, illegal panning and smuggling of gold and diamonds". [62]

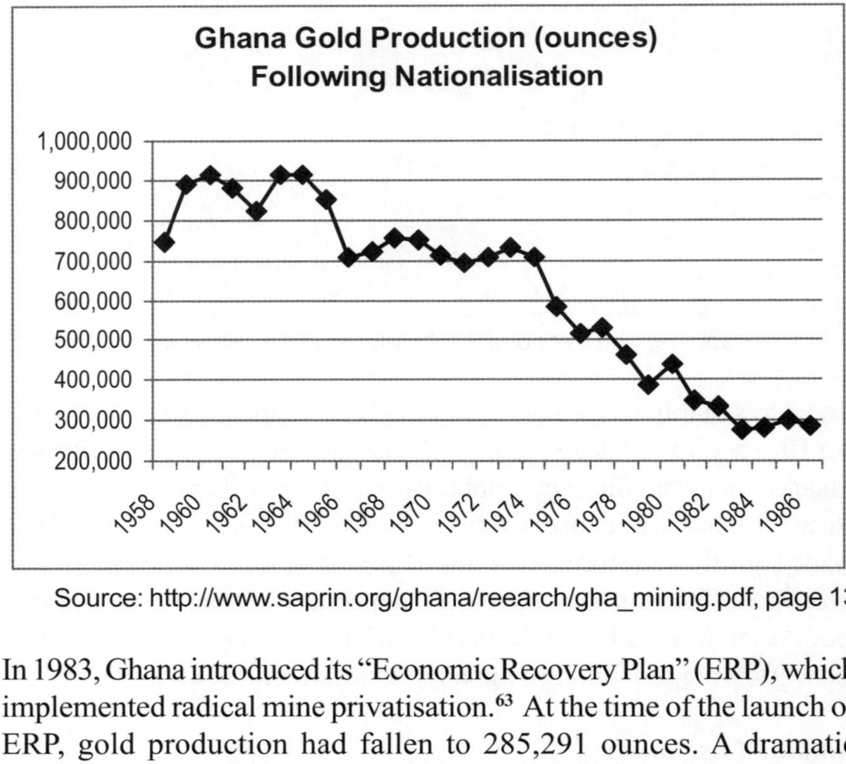


Source: http://www.saprin.org/ghana/reearch/gha_mining.pdf, page 13

In 1983, Ghana introduced its "Economic Recovery Plan" (ERP), which implemented radical mine privatisation.[63] At the time of the launch of ERP, gold production had fallen to 285,291 ounces. A dramatic improvement followed in the gold mining sector and rapid growth in annual gold production.

The contrast between the effects of nationalisation and privatisation on mining in Ghana is quite remarkable. After only 12 years, the privatised mines increased output from about 300,000 tons to approximately 2.5 million tons, an increase of over 700 per cent. In contrast, when mining operations were held in the hands of government, output declined steadily over a period of 29 years, from about 750,000 tons to about 280,000 tons.

Ghana's gold production increased to 2.9 million ounces in 2009. Since privatisation, the annual gold production in Ghana has increased more than 10 times over the last 27 years, and revenue reached $2.8 billion.

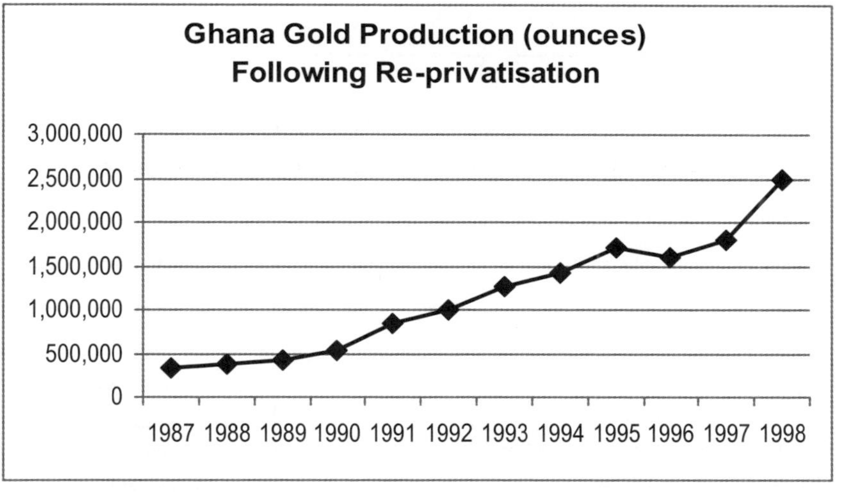


Source: http://www.saprin.org/ghana/reearch/gha_mining.pdf, page 16

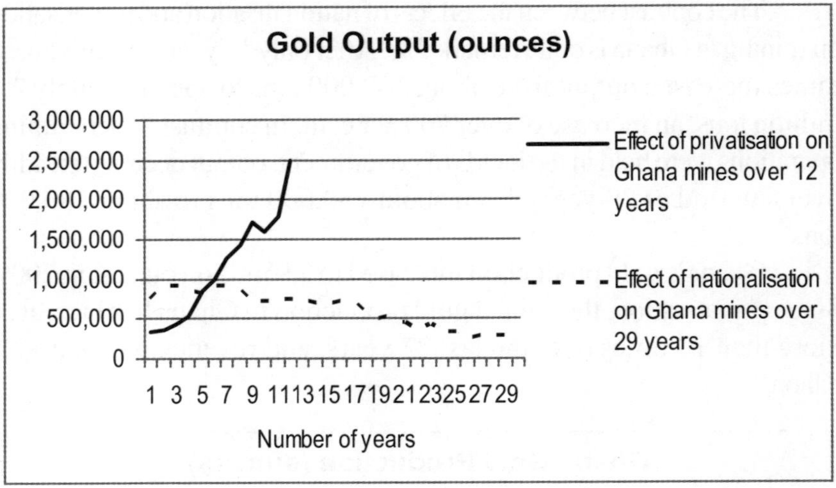

Gold Output (ounces)
3,000,000
2,500,000
2,000,000
1,500,000
1,000,000
500,000
0
1 3 5 7 9 11 13 15 17 19 21 23 25 27 29
Number of years
Effect of privatisation on Ghana mines over 12 years
Effect of nationalisation on Ghana mines over 29 years


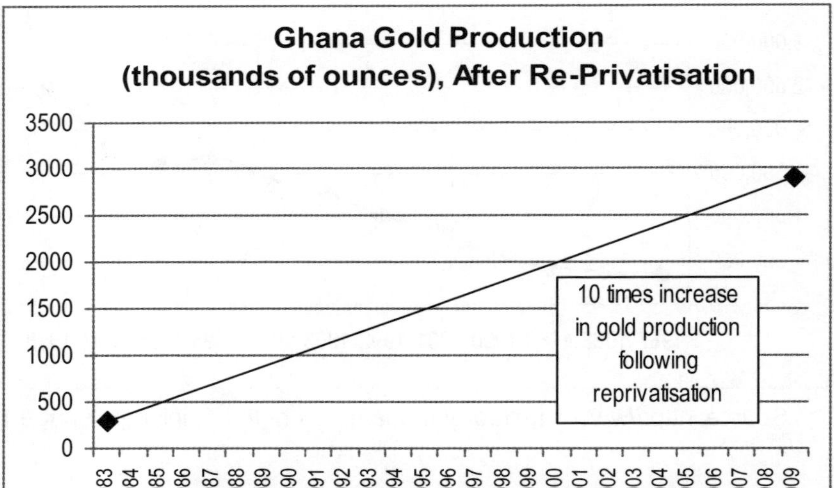

Ghana Gold Production (thousands of ounces), After Re-Privatisation
3500
3000
2500
2000
1500
1000
500
0
1983 1984 1985 1986 1987 1988 1989 1990 1991 1992 1993 1994 1995 1996 1997 1998 1999 2000 2001 2002 2003 2004 2005 2006 2007 2008 2009
10 times increase in gold production following reprivatisation

As a country, Ghana has benefited from the improvement in its mining situation. According to the US Geological Survey, "The contribution of Ghana's mining sector to the country's gross domestic product increased from 1.3% in 1991 to an average of about 5% in recent years. Export earnings from minerals averaged 35%, and the sector was one of the largest contributors to Government revenues through the payment of mineral royalties, employee income taxes, and corporate taxes". Growth in the mining sector also contributed substantially to a rise in per capita GDP (measured on a ppp basis), which increased from $449 in 1983 (in 2009 dollars) to $1571 in 2009, meaning Ghanaians, in 2009, were earning three and a half times more on average since the privatisation of mining.[64]

1 Thomas O'Malley, *Privatisation: A UK Success Story*, The Free Market Foundation, Johannesburg, 1998.
2 ibid.
3 ibid.
4 ibid.
5 ibid.
6 ibid.
7 ibid.
8 ANC Youth League Discussion Document, *Towards the Transfer of Mineral Wealth to the Ownership of the People as a Whole: A Perspective on Nationalization of Mines*, 2010.
9 Ronald T. Libby and Michael E. Woakes, *Nationalization and the Displacement of Development Policy in Zambia*, African Studies Review, vol. XXIII, no. 1, April 1980.
10 http://www.miningmx.com/news/base_metals/Zambia-targets-750000t-copper-this-year.htm.
11 Ronald T. Libby and Michael E. Woakes, op. cit.
12 ANC Youth League Discussion Document,op. cit.
13 D. Modise, *Management of Mineral Revenues: The Botswana Experience*. Presented at the Workshop on Growth and Diversification in Mineral Economies (organised by UNCTAD) in Cape Town, South Africa from 7-9 November 2000. Available at: http://www.unctad.org/infocomm/diversification/cape/pdf/modise.pdf.
14 Susan Anderson, *Botswana: Land of Paradoxes*, Mercatus Policy Series Country Brief No.1, Mercatus Center, 2005.

15 Botswana, National Accounts, 2007/08, Quarterly Report, December 2008. Available at: http://www.cso.gov.bw/images/stories/National_Accounts/na%2007-08%20report%20december%2008.pdf.

16 The poverty line is not an objective standard, but is set by the government according to six classes: food, clothing, personal items, household goods, shelter and miscellaneous items. National estimates are based on population weighted subgroup estimates from household surveys: 50 per cent of median income – 50 per cent of the median adjusted household disposable income.

17 Central Intelligence Agency, *The World Factbook: Botswana Country Profile*, 2010. Available at: https://www.cia.gov/library/publications/the-world-factbook/geos/bc.html.

18 Susan Anderson, op. cit.

19 ibid.

20 BIDPA Briefing, *Public Sector Reforms*, Botswana Institute for Development and Policy Analysis, 2004.

21 Franklin Tugwell, *The Politics of Oil in Venezuela,* Stanford University Press, 1975.

22 Central Intelligence Agency, *The World Factbook: Venezuela Country Profile*. Accessed: 9 November 2010. Available at: https://www.cia.gov/library/publications/the-world-factbook/geos/ve.html.

23 Gustavo Coronel, *The Nationalization of the Venezuelan Oil Industry,* Heath and Company, 1983.

24 Edward P. Stringham and John Levendis in James D. Gwartney, Joshua C. Hall, and Robert Lawson, *Economic Freedom of the World: 2010 Annual Report*, Chapter 6: The relationship between economic freedom and homicide, Fraser Institute, 2010.

25 Pamela Druckerman, 'Investors wince at likely Chavez victory – Venezuelan leader popular with the majority poor but not private sector', *Wall Street Journal*, 2000.

26 Marc Lifsher, 'In Venezuela, Chavez faces a crucial test – led by big business, energized opposition plans work stoppage', *Wall Street Journal*, 2001.

27 Bushman Bahree and Marc Lifsher, 'The other crisis facing Venezuela – its oil-output capacity is declining, and Chavez hasn't helped matters', *Wall Street Journal*, 2002.

28 Cesar Alvarez and Stephanie Hanson, *Venezuela's Oil-Based Economy*, Council on Foreign Relations, 2009. Available at: http://www.cfr.org/publication/12089 /venezuelas_oilbased_economy.html.

29 United Nations News Centre, *UN Labour Agency Discusses Repression in Myanmar, China, Colombia, Venezuela*, 2004. Accessed: 9 November 2010.

Available at: http://www.un.org/apps/news/storyAr.asp?NewsID=10242 &Cr=Myanmar& Cr1=&Kw1=Venezuela&Kw2=&Kw3=.

30 Cesar Alvarez and Stephanie Hanson, op. cit.

31 ibid.

32 Mary Anastasia O'Grady, 'Venezuela's monetary mayhem', *The Wall Street Journal*, 2010. Accessed: 9 November 2010. Available at: http://online.wsj.com/article/SB10001424052748703745904575247902269445166.html.

33 Cesar Alvarez and Stephanie Hanson, op. cit.

34 Mary Anastasia O'Grady, op. cit.

35 ibid.

36 Edward P. Stringham and John Levendis, op. cit.

37 Eyanir Chinea, Charlie Devereux and Andrew Cawthorne, 'Venezuela murder-rate quadrupled under Chavez: NGO', *Reuters*, 2010. Accessed: 10 November 2010. Available at: http://www.reuters.com/article/idUSTRE62A44A20100311.

38 Central Intelligence Agency, *The World Factbook: Bolivia Country Profile*, 2010.

39 Roberto Chang, Constantino Hevia and Norman Loayza, 'Privatization and nationalization cycles', National Bureau of Economic Research Working Paper 16126, 2010.

40 ibid.

41 ibid.

42 ibid.

43 ibid.

44 ibid.

45 Carin Zissis, *Bolivia's Nationalization of Oil and Gas*, Council on Foreign Relations, 2006.

46 ibid.

47 ibid.

48 http://en.wikipedia.org/wiki/G%C3%A9camines.

49 Dave Renton, David Seddon and Leo Zeilig, *The Congo: Plunder and Resistance*, pp.117-118.

50 Z. Moloo, *The Democratic Republic of Congo's Economic War: Investigating the Origin of Anonymous Commodities in the Global Capitalist System*, 2007. Accessed 3 December 2010. Available at Ota Benga Alliance: http://otabenga.org/files/moloo%20(c).pdf.

51 http://www.transnational-research.com/old-umhk.htm.

52 The name was changed from Zaire to the Democratic Republic of Congo in May 1997.

53 http://findarticles.com/p/articles/mi_qa3724/is_20080322/ai_n24952527/.

54 http://www.miningweekly.com/article/drc-sacks-gecamines-top-management-officials-2010-11-22.

55 http://www.mining-journal.com/production-and-markets/output-at-metorexs-ruashi-mine-hits-record.

56 http://internationalbusiness.wikia.com/wiki/Chilean_Nationalization_of_Copper.

57 Horace J. Stevens, *The Copper Handbook*, vol.8, p.1457, Houghton, Mich., 1908.

58 http://www.economist.com/node/17311933.

59 *The Economist*, 21 October 2010, 'Reviving Codelco'. Available at: http://www.economist.com/node/17311933.

60 http://www.saprin.org/ghana/research/gha_mining.pdf, p.11.

61 http://www.saprin.org/ghana/research/gha_mining.pdf.

62 J. Songsore, P.W.K. Yankson and G.K. Tsikata, *Mining and the Environment: Towards a Win-Win Strategy (A Study of the Tarkwa – Aboso – Nsuta Mining Complex in Ghana)*, Final Report, June 1994.

63 http://www.ghana-mining.org/ghweb/en/ma/mincom.html.

64 http://www.indexmundi.com/ghana/gdp_per_capita_(ppp).html.

Chapter 5

# Nationalisation and Black Advancement

## Executive Summary

In response to the ANCYL's proposal for the nationalisation of the mines this chapter looks at three questions relating to black advancement:

- To what extent have black people progressed due to freedom from apartheid?
- What is the value of the mining industry in South Africa and its contribution to GDP?
- What are the probable effects of nationalisation on black advancement?

Have the people who were previously disadvantaged by the policies of the apartheid regime gained from new-found freedom and new policies? According to a study on black advancement commenced in 2009 by the Free Market Foundation, blacks have made significant progress in various sectors of the economy. These include, but are not limited to, the JSE, the public sector, education, the financial sector, insurance, housing, etc.

## Black Advancement in the Public Sector

It was clear from the study on black advancement in the public sector that blacks and other previously disadvantaged employees in the public sector have benefited from the transition to democracy and now enjoy more employment opportunities than before. For example, blacks now make up more than 70 per cent of most government departments compared to 42 per cent in 1994.

## Black Advancement on the JSE

All studies on who owns South Africa's shares have revealed that black South African ownership of the country's financial assets is increasing.

Some 36 per cent of assets owned by South African individuals comprise shares listed on the JSE Securities Exchange; houses (primary property) make up around 33 per cent of South African assets; while the bank (money market), bonds and non-residential property make up another 31 per cent.

Of the total shares owned by South Africans, those owned by whites declined to 66 per cent in 2010 from 77 per cent in 2000, whereas Black ownership increased from 23 per cent in 2000 to 34 per cent in 2010. Both direct and indirect listed share ownership via vehicles such as pension and provident funds were included in the survey as well as long term insurance products.

Perhaps the biggest change in the last decade has been the explosion of foreign ownership of liquid South African assets. Along with many other emerging market countries, foreign investment into the equity market by foreign institutions has become very popular.

## The Mining Industry – Value and Contribution to GDP

According to Stats SA, since the transition to democracy, the South African GDP has increased from R779.43bn in 1994 to R1,271.72bn in 2008. The mining sector's contribution to GDP increased from R54.56bn in 1994 to R120.81bn in 2008, an increase in total from 7.0 per cent in 1994 to 9.5 per cent in 2008. The mining industry also accounted for 9 per cent of total fixed investment in the economy and for 13.3 per cent of total private-sector investment. According to the Chamber of Mines, if the multiplier effect is taken into account, mining helped generate 18 per cent of total investment in the economy.

Blacks made remarkable progress; now owning 23.5 per cent of the JSE after owning only 5 per cent in 1994, giving them a substantial stake in the mining industry. The number of pension funds and houses purchased by blacks has increased substantially. Blacks now own 37 per cent of retirement fund flows, a leap up from 23 per cent in 1995. Through investment funds and direct holdings blacks now own a significant percentage of the JSE.

## Probable Effects of Nationalisation on Black Advancement

Even though the intention is for many more blacks to be involved in mining, nationalisation would be the wrong route to take. Given that ownership by the state is not the same as ownership by the citizens of the state, nationalisation of the mines would actually mean a reduction in black ownership. Black participation in the mining sector would increase though if fostered through education, training, and entrepreneurship, and if they had easier access to finance. Assets take a long time to build, but, over time, in a free economy, this can be done by anyone of any race.

Chapter 5

# Nationalisation and Black Advancement

Vivian Abit Atud

## Introduction

Various authors and interest groups have assessed the ANCYL's proposal for the nationalisation of mines. Some have focused on its content and its assumptions, some on the economics of nationalisation, and others on the constitutionality of the proposal and its impact on the economy. This chapter seeks to examine the following research questions:

- To what extent have black people made progress due to freedom from apartheid?
- What is the value of the mining industry in South Africa and its contribution to GDP?
- What would be the probable effects of nationalisation on black advancement?

## Background

Racial segregation has been one of the defining characteristics of South Africa. Apartheid structures seriously limited the economic and social opportunities of non-Whites, allowing few from this vast group to participate in the formal[1] economy. Since the transition to democracy, new administrations have introduced various initiatives to adjust this skewed racial profile. From policy changes in personnel recruitment to how suppliers of goods and services are selected, and what type of enterprise development and social engagement is to be conducted, these administrations have taken a keen interest in reorganising South Africa's social, political, and economic structures.

But what have been the benefits of these actions? Have the people who were previously disadvantaged by the policies of the apartheid regime gained from new-found freedom and new policies? There appears to be no consensus regarding the extent to which or the mechanisms through which previously disadvantaged South Africans have benefited from the transition to democracy. Some authors argue that freedom from apartheid has not had a substantial impact on the social and economic development of black South Africans. Others hold the view that for these people to succeed, they need further government assistance through programmes such as Reconstruction and Development Programmes (RDP) and Black Economic Empowerment (BEE).[2] More recently, the ANCYL proposed that nationalisation (beginning with the mines) will extend benefits to all South Africans. Yet others believe that the core ingredients required for the true realisation of human potential are economic freedom, the development of a strong legal framework, a robust infrastructure, and human security.

According to a study on black advancement commenced in 2009 by the Free Market Foundation, blacks have made significant progress in various sectors of the economy. These include, but are not limited to, the JSE, the public sector, education, the financial sector, insurance, housing, etc.

## Black Advancement in the Public Sector

In 1994, the South African government consisted of 28 departments. During the past three administrations, the number fluctuated, with departments having to amend their titles and functions to accommodate the changes. In 2009, on his election, President Zuma and the current administration announced and put into action the establishment of more departments so that, today, the public service consists of 40 departments, an increase of 42 per cent.[3] Again, to accommodate this increase, many existing departments had to undergo a change in title and function.

It was clear from the study on black advancement in the public sector that blacks and other previously disadvantaged employees in this sector have benefited from the transition to democracy and now enjoy more employment opportunities than before. For example, blacks now make up more than 70 per cent of most public departments compared to 42 per cent, which was the case in 1994.

## Black Advancement on the JSE

All studies on who owns South Africa's shares have revealed that black South African ownership of the country's financial assets is increasing.

Some 36 per cent of assets owned by South African individuals comprise shares listed on the JSE Securities Exchange; houses (primary property) make up around 33 per cent of South African assets; while the bank (money market), bonds and non-residential property make up another 31 per cent.

Chart 1: South African Asset Make Up

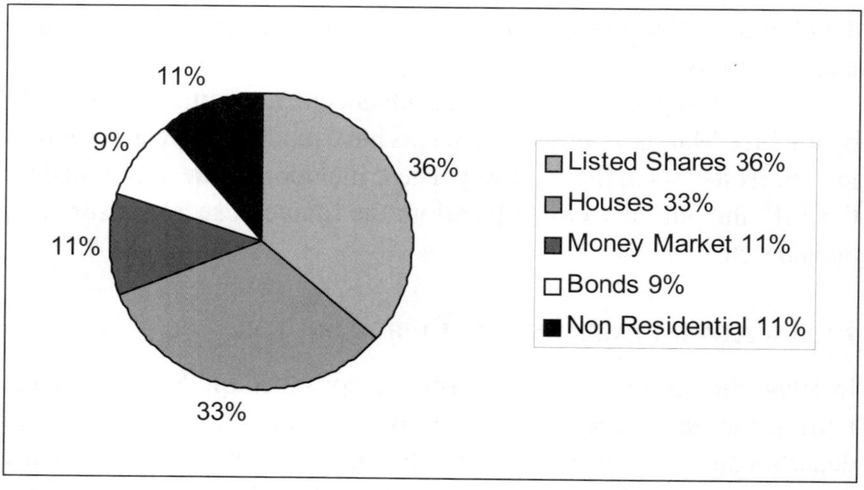

### *Share Market Including Foreign and State Ownership*

Leaving out cross ownership between companies and looking at only individual and institutional share ownership: (Institutions are pension funds, unit trusts, long term insurers and medical schemes and the like who keep money on behalf of individuals):

Table 1: Ownership of the JSE by Segment Including Foreign

| | Black | Coloured | Indian | White | Foreign | State |
|---|---|---|---|---|---|---|
| **2000** | 14.9% | 4.7% | 2.3% | 71.4% | 5.8% | 1.0% |
| **2010** | 17.4% | 3.0% | 2.5% | 44.5% | 31.1% | 1.5% |

Source: Economists.co.za

Perhaps the biggest change in the last decade has been the explosion of foreign ownership of liquid South African assets. Along with many other emerging market countries, foreign investment into the equity market by foreign institutions has become very popular. Black ownership increased slightly from 22 per cent to around 23 per cent while white ownership declined systematically from 71 per cent in 2000 to 45 per cent.

### *JSE Ownership by South African Individuals by Race*

The South African share ownership can also be described without taking into account foreign or state ownership.

While the majority of shares in 2010 are still owned by whites, this percentage has steadily declined to 66 per cent from 77 per cent in 2000, and demonstrates that share ownership by previously disadvantaged South Africans is rising. Both direct and indirect listed share ownership via vehicles such as pension and provident funds were included in the survey as well as long term insurance products. Progress has been slow, but steady. Black ownership of listed equities has risen from 16 per cent in 2000 to 25.8 per cent. Indians now own 3.7 per cent of listed shares, up from 2.5 per cent ten years ago, while ownership by Coloureds has declined from 5.0 per cent to 4.5 per cent. Total Black, Coloured and Indian share ownership increased from 23.5 per cent in 2000 to 34 per cent in 2010.

Chart 2: Ownership of the JSE by South African Individuals by Race

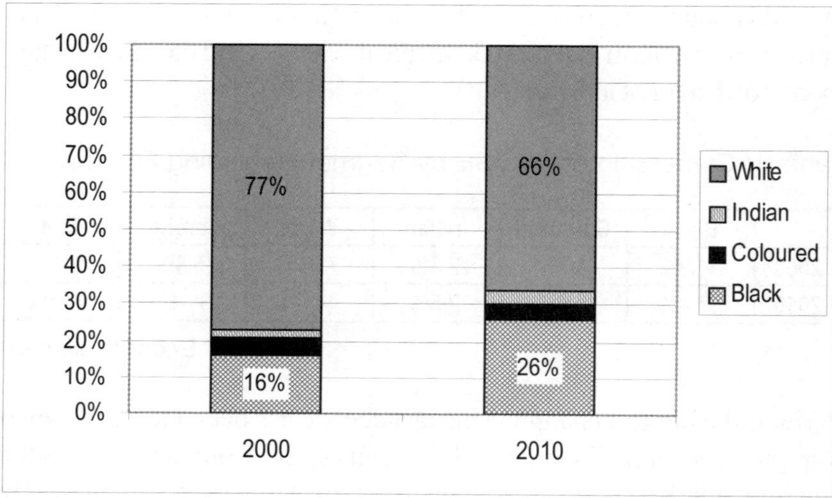


Figures have been sourced from data published by Statistics South Africa (Stats SA), the SA Reserve Bank (SARB), Who Owns Whom and SA Advertising Research Foundation (AMPS). Using this information, a close approximation of the extent of shareholding of JSE-listed companies by race was made. Data from different sources were crosschecked to ensure greater robustness of the information.

The total level of the JSE market capitalisation was taken from the SARB Quarterly Bulletin. The cross-holdings and treasury shares were then stripped out to derive the shares held by individuals and institutions. Foreign ownership was also removed using information from Who Owns Whom as well as from SARB, to determine a figure for Domestic Investable Shares.

Use was made of data included in SA Censuses, The Labour Force Survey and AMPS which indicate both the racial breakdown of the population who purchase retirement products and pension funds, as well as the ownership levels of a variety of financial assets including retirement funds and life policies. One of the assumptions made was that people with the same income would save at the average rate for the specific income level.

Table 2: Current Contributions to a Pension or Retirement Fund by Race

| Current Income and Race Weighted Flows | | | | | |
|---|---|---|---|---|---|
| | Black | Coloured | Indian | White | BCI* |
| 1995 | 15% | 6% | 2% | 77% | 23% |
| 1996 | 16% | 6% | 2% | 76% | 24% |
| 1997 | 17% | 6% | 2% | 75% | 25% |
| 1998 | 18% | 6% | 2% | 74% | 26% |
| 1999 | 19% | 6% | 2% | 73% | 27% |
| 2000 | 24% | 6% | 2% | 69% | 32% |
| 2001 | 27% | 9% | 1% | 63% | 37% |
| 2002 | 27% | 5% | 2% | 67% | 33% |
| 2003 | 27% | 5% | 3% | 65% | 35% |
| 2004 | 31% | 4% | 3% | 61% | 39% |
| 2005 | 31% | 7% | 5% | 58% | 43% |
| 2006 | 35% | 5% | 9% | 51% | 49% |
| 2007 | 42% | 4% | 3% | 51% | 49% |
| 2008 | 42% | 4% | 3% | 51% | 49% |
| 2009 | 43% | 2% | 4% | 51% | 49% |
| 2010 | 39% | 3% | 5% | 53% | 47% |

Source: AMPS, Quarterly Labour Force Survey (QLFS), General Household Survey (GHS).
*BCI: Black, Coloured and Indian

Retirement funds and long term insurance are the biggest investors on the JSE – not only by mandated funds but also overall, and in some years make up over 50 per cent of the total investable shares of the JSE. (After company cross-holdings and foreign shares have been subtracted.)

It was important to correctly establish the contribution to retirement funds and pension funds by race and income. Using both AMPS and labour force survey data it was possible to determine these figures fairly accurately as more than 538,000 South Africans were asked about their income levels as well as whether they contribute to a retirement fund.

These figures provided high-quality estimates of ownership of financial retirement or pension assets by race, as they referred back as far as 1995.

This shows an encouraging picture, but clearly there is room for further progress. Ten years ago, only 24 per cent of the purchases on the JSE were being made on behalf of black owners. That figure has now risen to almost 40 per cent. Flows from Indians have also witnessed a strong rise, from less than 2 per cent in 2000, to the current 5.3 per cent. By contrast, white purchasing has slipped to 53 per cent in 2010 from 69 per cent in 2000. (These figures are represented in Table 2.)

Similar questions were asked in AMPS on Unit trusts, direct share ownership and a host of other financial products over the years. Using both net contribution rates and share market growth rates we were able to get a clear trend over time in the ownership of JSE shares over the last 15 years.

We then approximated the ongoing contributions to each of the asset classes by race, which gives an indication of the future trend that overall ownership is expected to take. Contributions by both employers and employees into retirement funds were taken into account using SARB data.

Table 3: Racial Shares in Retirement Funds (1995 to 2010)

| Share by Race of Retirement Funds | | | | | |
|---|---|---|---|---|---|
| | **Black** | **Coloured** | **Indian** | **White** | **BCI*** |
| **1995** | 15% | 6% | 2% | 77% | 23% |
| **1996** | 16% | 6% | 2% | 76% | 24% |
| **1997** | 17% | 6% | 2% | 75% | 25% |
| **1998** | 18% | 6% | 2% | 74% | 26% |
| **1999** | 18% | 6% | 2% | 74% | 26% |
| **2000** | 19% | 6% | 2% | 73% | 27% |
| **2001** | 20% | 6% | 2% | 72% | 28% |
| **2002** | 20% | 6% | 2% | 72% | 28% |
| **2003** | 20% | 6% | 2% | 71% | 29% |
| **2004** | 22% | 6% | 2% | 70% | 30% |
| **2005** | 23% | 6% | 3% | 68% | 32% |
| **2006** | 25% | 6% | 4% | 65% | 35% |
| **2007** | 27% | 6% | 4% | 64% | 36% |
| **2008** | 27% | 6% | 4% | 64% | 36% |
| **2009** | 28% | 5% | 4% | 63% | 37% |
| **2010** | 28% | 5% | 4% | 63% | 37% |

Source: AMPS, Quarterly Labour Force Survey (QLFS),
General Household Survey (GHS).
Income flows for retirement funds and long-term insurance
funds were also taken into account as well as
equity market movements over the years.
*BCI: Black, Coloured and Indian

The total collective value of the market cap for South Africans including indirect shares is nearly R3.3 trillion.

Table 4: Total Individual Ownership of the JSE by Race

| Total JSE by Race | | | | | |
|---|---|---|---|---|---|
| | Black | Coloured | Indian | White | BCI* |
| 2000 | 16.0% | 5.0% | 2.5% | 76.5% | 23.5% |
| 2010 | 25.8% | 4.5% | 3.7% | 66.0% | 34.0% |

Source: Economists.co.za from AMPS, QLFS, GHS, etc. for individuals only after foreign shares and state share have been excluded.
* BCI: Black, Coloured and Indian

Table 5: Mandated Funds Only Market Capitalisation by Race

| Mandated Funds by Race | | | | | |
|---|---|---|---|---|---|
| | Black | Coloured | Indian | White | BCI* |
| 2000 | 19% | 6% | 2% | 73% | 27% |
| 2010 | 28% | 5% | 4% | 63% | 37% |

Source: Economists.co.za from AMPS, QLFS, GHS, etc. "rounded" for individuals only after foreign shares and state share have been excluded.
* BCI: Black, Coloured and Indian

Table 6: Direct Share Market Capitalisation by Race

| Direct Retail Shares by Race | | | | | |
|---|---|---|---|---|---|
| | Black | Coloured | Indian | White | BCI* |
| 2000 | 9% | 3% | 2% | 86% | 14% |
| 2010 | 19% | 3% | 3% | 76% | 24% |

Source: Economists.co.za from AMPS "rounded" for individuals only after foreign shares and state share have been excluded.
* BCI: Black, Coloured and Indian

The majority of share ownership is via mandated funds in South Africa and the composition of the mandated funds is about 63 per cent white- and 37 per cent black-owned. Mandated funds make up 72 per cent of South African ownership.

Direct ownership is still majority owned by whites with about a 76 per cent share but broader black ownership has increased to around 25 per cent today. Direct ownership makes up about 28 per cent of the South African shares. Therefore since the transition to democracy, black South Africans are making significant progress in owning various financial assets and also investing on the JSE. Nationalisation may hamper this self-earned progress by increasing dependency on the state instead of the individual creativity that has been seen over the past 16 years.

## The Mining Industry – Value and Contribution to GDP

According to Stats SA, since the transition to democracy, the South African GDP has increased from R779.43bn in 1994 to R1,271.72bn in 2008. The mining sector contribution to GDP increased from R54.56bn in 1994 to R120.81bn in 2008, increasing in total from 7.0 per cent in 1994 to 9.5 per cent in 2008.

Chart 4: South African GDP and Mining Sector Contribution to GDP (1994-2008)

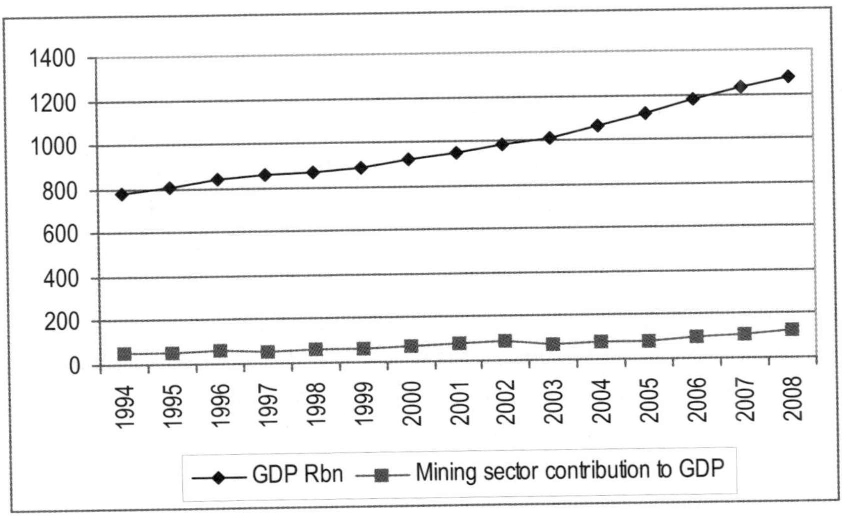


Source: Data from Stats SA, chart by author

The mining industry also accounted for 9 per cent of total fixed investment in the economy and for 13.3 per cent of total private-sector investment. According to the Chamber of Mines, if the multiplier effect is taken into account, mining helped generate 18 per cent of total investment in the economy.

The industry continued to act as a magnet for investment in South Africa, according to the Chamber. At the end of December 2008, the mining sector accounted for R1.4 trillion, or 31 per cent, of the value of the JSE. Given that mines make up 31 per cent of the value of the JSE of which blacks own a substantial 23.5 per cent, there is already significant ownership of mines by blacks without any need for nationalisation. This ownership is still increasing. If the call for nationalisation is heeded, the overall result will be a decrease in black ownership.

Government's inability to manage businesses is evident from the performance of State-Owned Enterprises (SOEs). In South Africa, SOEs have generally been economically unsuccessful and have high levels of borrowing, which raise the overall level of the borrowing requirement in the public sector. This results directly in high interest payments that affect the profitability of SOEs and their capacity to grasp development opportunities. State-owned diamond mine Alexkor has suffered major losses and the company's contribution to government revenue and cash flow has been minimal, if not a drain. It has also had no, or very little, impact on poverty and inequality. Therefore to continue to sustain the current levels of black advancement in all sectors, business, including mines, should be run by private individuals who possess the required resources and capabilities. The result will be more blacks will continue to build assets for themselves and the levels of poverty and black unemployment will decrease.

Blacks have already made remarkable progress; now owning 23 per cent of the JSE (34 per cent if foreign and state-owned shares are excluded) up from 5 per cent in 1994. There have been remarkable increases in the purchase of pension funds and houses by blacks, now owning 37 per cent of retirement funds, up from 23 per cent in 1995.

## Probable Effects of Nationalisation on Black Advancement

Even though many more blacks may wish to be involved in mining, nationalisation would be the wrong route to take. Given that ownership by the state is not the same as ownership by the citizens of the state, nationalisation of the mines would actually mean a reduction in black ownership. Black participation in the mining sector would increase though if fostered through education, training, and entrepreneurship, and if they had easier access to finance.

Assets take a long time to build, but, over time, in a free economy, this can be done by anyone of any race.

1 Formal economy refers to all economic activities that are officially registered to operate and counted/recorded in government statistics, while informal businesses are often not registered, do not pay tax, and yet contribute to the economy.
2 Broad definition of Black includes Indian and Coloured.
3 See http://www.info.gov.za/aboutgovt/dept.htm.

Chapter 6

# Rewards of Economic Freedom

## Executive Summary

The world's most successful countries generally achieve high and stable economic growth, sound legal systems, security of persons and their property, sound money, freedom to trade, low rates of unemployment, minimum levels of crime and violence, an absence of poverty, high average incomes, low taxes, open opportunity, political and civil liberties, and peace. Without fail, the countries that rank highest for providing their citizens with these desirable conditions also rank highest on the indices of economic freedom.

Building a successful, wealthy, and peaceful nation requires patience, courage, tenacity, and above all, policies based on well-founded and proven fundamental principles of law and economics.

The *Index of Economic Freedom* published by the Wall Street Journal and the Heritage Foundation, USA, and *Economic Freedom of the World* (EFW) published annually by the Fraser Institute, Canada, in co-operation with the Economic Freedom Network, are the best known measures of economic freedom.

## Economic Freedom and its Rewards

Nations in the top quartile of the EFW index had an average per-capita GDP of $32,744 in 2007, compared to $3,858 for those nations in the bottom quartile measured in constant 2005 international dollars.

Moreover, the average income of the poorest 10 per cent of the population in the most-free quartile was $8,474 compared to $910 for those in the least-free quartile measured in constant 2005 international dollars. Contrary to popular opinion, the poor get richer fastest in economically free countries. People in nations in the most-free quartile also report a much higher level of life satisfaction of 7.5 out of 10 as opposed to people in the least free economies who report a life satisfaction of 4.7 out of 10.

Without voluntary exchange and entrepreneurial activity co-ordinated through markets, modern living standards would be impossible. A trend towards greater economic freedom results in increased economic growth while the reverse trend reduces growth.

## Economic Freedom and Unemployment

In the EFW 2010 annual report, Horst Feldmann from the University of Bath examines the relationship between economic freedom and unemployment. According to his regression results, more economic freedom appears to reduce unemployment. The magnitude of the effect seems to be substantial, especially among young people. Given the large costs of unemployment and the enormous number of jobless people in South Africa, particularly in the wake of the financial and economic crisis where an estimated one million jobs were lost, the South African government should seriously consider increasing economic freedom as a means of reducing unemployment.

## The Relationship between Economic Freedom and Homicide

One of the recent negative correlations to be identified is the relationship between economic freedom and crime. In the EFW 2010 Annual Report

Stringham and Levendis state, "Adam Smith (1776) and Frederic Bastiat (1850)… believed that even if people pursue their self-interests under a market system, individuals can only gain by working for their fellow men. They argued that, even if people have different ends, the prospect of mutual gains through exchange promotes cooperation". Stringham and Levendis find that economic freedom and homicide rates are negatively correlated. In other words high levels of economic freedom are associated with a more peaceful society. Increase economic freedom, they suggest, and the figures show that the number of homicides will decrease.

## Effect of Size of Government on the Welfare of Citizens

Where governments absorb a greater share of GDP and dominate a greater part of the economy, incomes tend to be lower. Increases in the extent to which government takes control of economic resources, whether by taxation or nationalisation, bring about reductions in the consumer sovereignty that should reign in a healthy economy.

## Nationalisation and Economic Freedom

An increased role for governments in their economies has not proved to be beneficial to the long-term interests of their citizens as measured by GDP per capita. In South Africa, nationalisation of the mines would increase the government's role considerably, but, as the EFW data shows, is likely to have detrimental rather than positive consequences for the country's economy.

Chapter 6

# Rewards of Economic Freedom

Eustace Davie
& Jasson Urbach

NATIONALISATION

A list of the desirable conditions for the establishment of a peaceful and contented nation is likely to include: high and stable economic growth, a sound legal system, security of persons and their property, sound money, freedom to trade, a low unemployment rate, minimum levels of crime and violence, an absence of poverty, high average incomes, low taxes, open opportunity, political and civil liberties, and peace. Experience has shown that these features have been achieved, to a greater or lesser degree, by the world's most successful countries.

Without fail, the countries that rank highest for providing their citizens with these desirable conditions also rank highest on the indices of economic freedom. This is no coincidence. Building a successful, wealthy, and peaceful nation requires patience, courage, tenacity, and above all, policies based on well-founded and proven fundamental principles of law and economics.

There are two annual publications that measure economic freedom. They are the *Index of Economic Freedom* published by the Wall Street Journal and the Heritage Foundation, USA, and *Economic Freedom of the World* (EFW) published by the Fraser Institute, Canada, in co-operation with the Economic Freedom Network. The Free Market Foundation, a member of the Economic Freedom Network, publishes a South African edition of EFW. Both publications resulted from a challenge issued by Milton Friedman to a meeting of classical liberals in the mid-1980s to measure countries' levels of economic freedom and prove their contention that greater economic freedom improves the lives of their citizens.

EFW measures the degree to which the policies and institutions of the 141 countries surveyed support economic freedom. The foundations of economic freedom are personal choice, voluntary exchange, freedom to compete and security of privately owned property. Forty-two data points are used to construct a summary index and to measure the degree of economic freedom in five broad areas: (1) size of government; (2) legal structure and security of property rights; (3) access to sound money; (4) freedom to trade internationally; and (5) regulation of credit, labour and business.[1]

## Economic Freedom and its Rewards

One of the key objectives in compiling EFW is to establish whether relationships exist between economic freedom and economic growth and wealth creation. The findings unambiguously support the fact that economic freedom is strongly related to prosperity and growth – countries that are economically free tend to grow faster and be more prosperous.[2] More specifically, nations in the top quartile of the economic freedom index had an average per-capita GDP of $32,744 in 2007, compared to $3,858 for those nations in the bottom quartile measured in constant 2005 international dollars (see Economic Freedom and Income per Capita graph below).

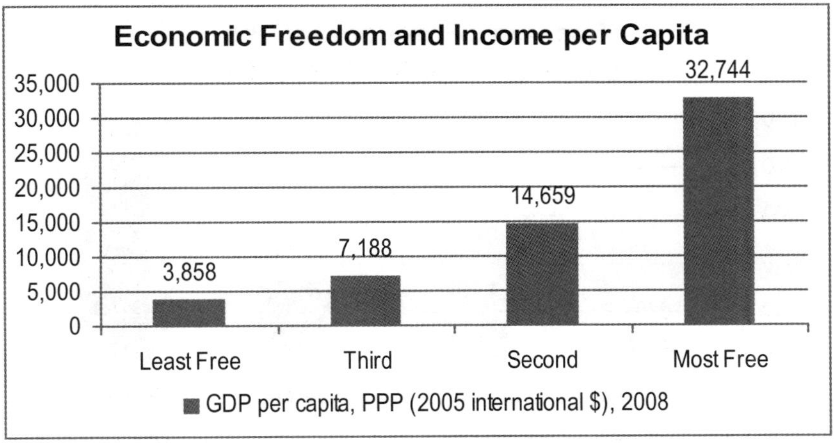


Sources: Fraser Institute, *Economic Freedom of the World: 2010 Annual Report*; World Bank, *World Development Indicators*

Moreover, the average income of the poorest 10 per cent of the population in the most-free quartile was $8,474 compared to $910 for those in the least-free quartile measured in constant 2005 international dollars (see Economic Freedom and the Income Level of the Poorest 10% graph below). Contrary to popular opinion, in economically free countries, while the rich get richer, the poor do not get poorer; the evidence shows that the poor get richer too and they get richer fastest in economically free countries. People in nations in the most-free quartile also report a much higher level of life satisfaction of 7.5 out of 10 as opposed to people in the least free economies who report a life satisfaction of 4.7 out of 10.

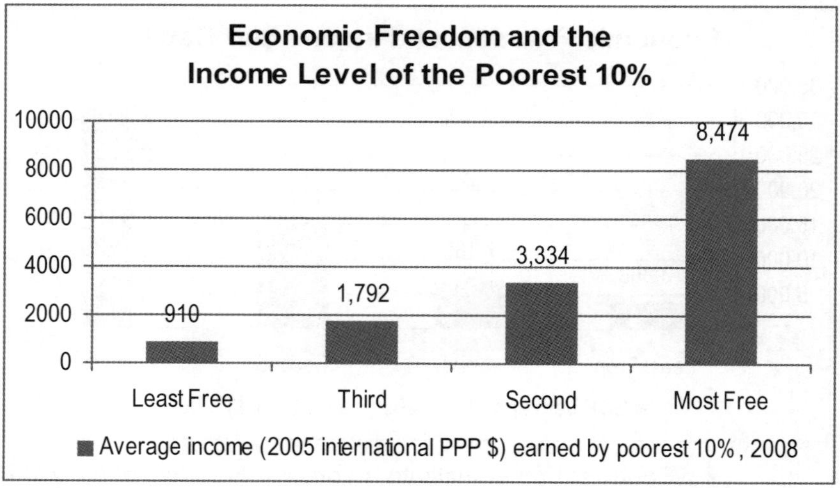


Sources: Fraser Institute, *Economic Freedom of the World: 2010 Annual Report*; World Bank, *World Development Indicators*

More importantly, life expectancy is nearly 20 years longer in countries with the most economic freedom than it is in those with the least. For countries in the top quartile of the index, life expectancy is 79.3 years but a mere 59.9 years for those countries falling into the bottom quartile of the index (see Economic Freedom and Life Expectancy graph below).

As Adam Smith, Milton Friedman and Friedrich Hayek stressed, freedom of exchange and market coordination provide the fuel for economic progress. Without voluntary exchange and entrepreneurial activity co-ordinated through markets, modern living standards would be impossible.

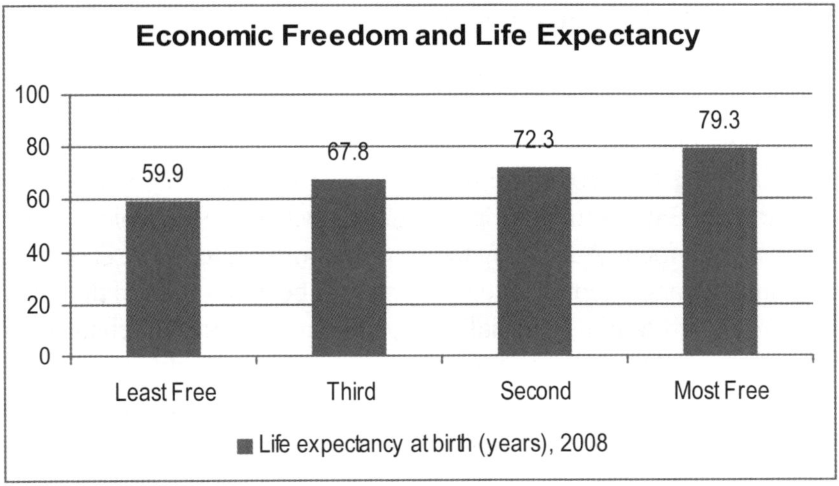


Sources: Fraser Institute, *Economic Freedom of the World: 2010 Annual Report*; World Bank, *World Development Indicators*

This notion is supported by looking at the highest ranked countries over the past few years. In the 2010 report Hong Kong received a rating of 9.05 out of 10, closely followed by Singapore (8.70), New Zealand (8.27), Switzerland (8.08) and Chile (8.03). The remaining five positions in the top ten were held by the United States (7.96), Canada (7.95), Australia (7.90), Mauritius (7.82) and the United Kingdom (7.81). The majority of these countries appear in the top ten of the United Nations' Human Development Index. The common denominator is that all of these nations have ensured high standards of living and high rates of growth by applying free market policies.

EFW unequivocally presents the findings that governments wishing to see their economies grow must take the direction of change towards economically freer societies seriously. A trend towards greater economic freedom results in increased economic growth while the reverse trend reduces growth. The consequences may not be immediately apparent but they are no less certain.

## Economic Freedom and Unemployment

According to the latest statistics from Stats SA, there are currently 7.3 million unemployed people in South Africa and the rate of unemployment is 36.6 per cent.

In the EFW 2010 annual report, Horst Feldmann from the University of Bath examines the relationship between economic freedom and unemployment. According to his regression results, more economic freedom appears to reduce unemployment. The magnitude of the effect seems to be substantial, especially among young people. Given the large costs of unemployment and the enormous number of jobless people in South Africa, particularly in the wake of the financial and economic crisis where an estimated 1 million jobs were lost, the South African government should seriously consider increasing economic freedom as a means of reducing unemployment.

The negative consequences associated with unemployment not only affect the individual and their family and friends, but also impact on society at large. People who are unemployed are forced to 'borrow' money from family and friends but if unemployment is chronic, this money eventually becomes a 'gift' when the unemployed person remains in a position where they are unable to repay the loan. This 'borrowing' is far from costless as it puts personal relationships under increasing strain. The individual suffers the emotional stress related to being unemployed and the 'lender' suffers personal financial loss. Indeed, Linn *et al.* (1985) report unemployment has a negative impact on the health of affected individuals. According to their study, symptoms of depression and anxiety in men in America are significantly greater in the unemployed than in the employed. Similarly, using a sample of German blue-collar workers, Frese and Mohr (1987) find that prolonged or repeated unemployment leads to depression.

According to EFW, South Africa ranks among the poorest in the world on labour market regulation. On minimum wages, South Africa has a rating of 4.40 out of a possible 10 and in the area of flexibility in hiring and firing a very low rating of 2.48.

## The Relationship between Economic Freedom and Homicide

As we have seen above, higher levels of economic freedom are associated with a number of positive outcomes in society. One of the recent negative correlations to be identified is the relationship between economic freedom and crime. In the EFW 2010 Annual Report Stringham and Levendis state, "Adam Smith (1776) and Frederic Bastiat (1850)… believed that even if people pursue their self-interests under a market system, individuals can only gain by working for their fellow men. They argued that, even if people have different ends, the prospect of mutual gains through exchange promotes cooperation". Stringham and Levendis analyse data from countries across the globe for which there is reliable information on economic freedom and various measures of conflict. They use this data to investigate whether measures of market freedom are positively or negatively correlated with measures of conflict. They considered homicide to be the best proxy of conflict because various crime reporting statistics may differ by country. Stringham and Levendis find that economic freedom and homicide rates are negatively correlated. In other words high levels of economic freedom are associated with a more peaceful society.

The authors examined the impact of declines and increases in economic freedom ratings on homicide rates in various countries during the period 1990 to 2007. A decline from 5.63 to 4.35 (out of 10) in Venezuela's EFW rating coincided with an increase in the homicide rate from just above 10 to 48 per 100,000. Colombia's EFW rating rose from 5.19 to 6.13 and the homicide rate declined from 24 per 100,000 to 17. For Latvia the EFW score went from 5.30 to 7.23 and the homicide rate from 11.5 to 7.7. Lithuania improved its EFW score from 5.21 in 1995 to 7.41 in 2007 and homicides declined from 68 to 37. South Africa's EFW score improved from 5.46 in 1990 to 6.90 in 2007 and homicides declined from 68 to 37 per 100,000.

The researchers reached the conclusion that, "From a normative point of view, the findings indicate a previously unconsidered influence on homicide and a possible way to decrease it." Increase economic freedom, they suggest, and the figures show that the number of homicides will decline.

## Effect of Size of Government on the Welfare of Citizens

The following graph reflects the correlation between the size of government (as measured by Area 1 of the EFW index) for the top and bottom ten ranked countries (and South Africa) and their GDPs per capita. The graph indicates that where governments absorb a greater share of GDP and dominate a greater part of the economy, incomes tend to be lower. This measure of economic freedom (Area 1: Size of government) is intended to determine and compare "the extent to which countries rely on the political process to allocate resources, goods and services".[3] According to the authors, when government spending increases relative to spending by individuals, households and businesses, government decision-making is substituted for personal choice and economic freedom is reduced".[4]

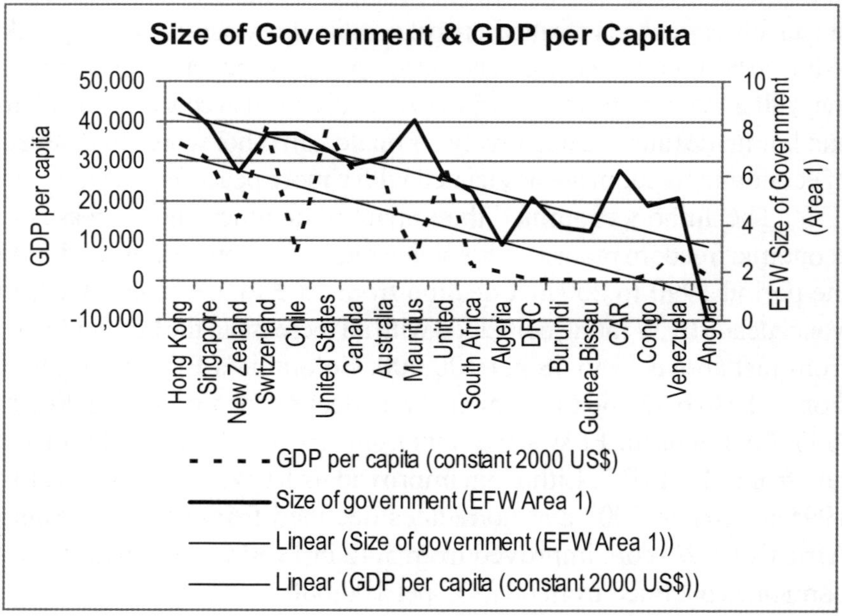


Sources: Fraser Institute, *Economic Freedom of the World: 2010 Annual Report*; World Bank, *World Development Indicators*

Another important factor is the extent to which private providers, rather than government enterprises, produce goods and services. Government providers of goods and services do not respond to the demands of consumers in the same way that competitive private enterprises are compelled to do if they wish to remain in business. Increases in the extent to which government takes control of economic resources, whether by taxation or nationalisation, bring about reductions in the consumer sovereignty that should reign in a healthy economy. Politicians may believe that they can construct a better delivery process than private firms but the fact that they are not responsive to consumers makes such a belief ill-founded.

## Nationalisation and Economic Freedom

Evidence from around the world has shown that an increased role for governments in their economies has not proved to be beneficial to the long-term interests of their citizens as measured by GDP per capita. In South Africa, nationalisation of the mines would increase the government's role considerably, but, as the EFW data shows, is likely to have detrimental rather than positive consequences for the country's economy.

South Africa's EFW rating for the component "government enterprises and investment" fell from a creditable 8.0 (out of a possible 10) in 1995 to 4.0 in 2008. In the construction of the EFW index "when a substantial number of SOEs operated in many sectors, including manufacturing, and government investment was between 40% and 50% of the total, countries received a rating of 4."

The reduced "Size of Government" rating has played a considerable role in South Africa's slide from 48th place on the EFW index to 82nd. As the direction of change has proved to be an accurate predictor of economic improvement or decline in the countries measured, exacerbating that deterioration by nationalisation should be avoided by a government intent on improving the lives of its citizens.

1 James D. Gwartney; Joshua Hall, and Robert Lawson (2010) *Economic Freedom of the World: 2010 Annual Report*, Fraser Institute. Available at: http://www.freetheworld.com/release.html.

2 ibid.

3 James D. Gwartney; Joshua Hall, and Robert Lawson (2010) *Economic Freedom of the World: 2010 Annual Report*, Fraser Institute. Available at: http://www.freetheworld.com/release.html.

4 ibid.